The Executive's Guide to Winning Presentations

Herman Holtz

John Wiley & Sons, Inc.

New York • Chichester • Brisbane • Toronto • Singapore

Copyright © 1991 by Herman Holtz.
Published by John Wiley & Sons, Inc.

Library of Congress Cataloging-in-Publication Data

Holtz, Herman.
    The executive's guide to winning presentations / Herman Holtz.
        p.   cm.
    Includes index.
    ISBN 0-471-52478-6. — ISBN 0-471-54196-6 (pbk.)
    1. Business presentations.   I. Title.
    HF5718.22.H65   1991
    658.4'52—dc20   90-32024
                                                   CIP

Printed in the United States of America

91 92 10 9 8 7 6 5 4 3 2 1

Foreword

I am honored to be asked by my talented friend, Herman Holtz, to write the Foreword for this important book. I invite you to think about the word "present" in the title. If pronounced with the emphasis on the first syllable, the meaning is to "be there"—completely—for your listeners . . . to focus entirely on them. To be and have presence is the most important part of any presentation. Presenters who have this winning quality are like those with Barrie's description of those with charm: "If you don't have it, it doesn't matter what else you have. If you do have it, you don't need anything else."

Why don't some presenters have presence? Some are overcome with fear. The most frequently asked questions at our professional speaking seminars is "How can I overcome fear?"

Our students tell us that their hands shake and their hearts pound as they stand to make a presentation. They perspire and their mouths become so dry their lips stick to their teeth. They are terrified that they will go blank and forget their entire presentation. Sound familiar?

The way to banish fear is to replace it with a burning passionate desire to present your important knowledge, helpful story, and "delicious" material to the hungry people before you. Wait a minute: "Hungry," you ask?

Yes, I mean exactly that. Fill you mind with wanting to help your audience, and your fear clicks off. The brilliant light of caring about the people you are there for, far more than you care about yourself, clicks on like a huge fluorescent fixture and illuminates your mind. You step forward with a presence that fills the room.

Fear is the absence of light, like a pitch black room. Fear is composed of thinking of yourself. "Are my clothes perfect? Could my hair look better? What about my voice—too low, too high? Should I gesture with big movements or little small ones? What if I forget one sentence?" Some presenters actually believe that everyone in the room has a script and is going to grade them on not leaving out a single word! When you focus on "I, me myself," you turn off the light.

Here is a mental exercise I use that has helped me and thousands of other presenters I have taught. As I stand off-stage I think, "My hair, clothes, and preparation are great. I am ready. My introducer has prepared and will bring me on exactly the way we rehearsed."

Then I look at the audience and I visualize each of them holding an empty bowl—like the children in Charles Dickens' story *Oliver*. I see that they are hungry. Then I visualize a large, unlimited tray of the most delicious food you can imagine in my hands.

I have gathered and prepared the food. It is the audience's favorite. I am so eager to feed them, I eagerly step out on the stage, smile at them, and call out mentally:

> There you are! I am so glad you came!
> I am the one you have been waiting for!
> Here I have scrumptious thoughts for you,
> Enjoy, enjoy, enjoy!

They smile back at me, and we begin! I love them with all my heart. No room for fear because they love me back, and we make a beautiful light together.

DOTTIE WALTERS
Walters International Speakers Bureau
Glendora, California

Preface

Why should you learn to make an effective presentation? What does it mean to you? What will it do for you?

It can become an important element in your career success, and may even be a decisive one. That is true whether you are employed by an organization or are self-employed. It is true whether you are an executive, engineer, staff professional, marketer, sales representative, teacher, consultant, or in any of many other possible positions. Customers, clients, associates, and employers are likely to judge you far more on the basis of how effective a presentation you can make to subordinates, peers, superiors, clients, prospects, or others than on how effective you are at your specific job.

It is also quite likely that you will find yourself called upon often to deliver presentations of many kinds and on many occasions—from the keynote speech at a convention to a formal marketing presentation. But there are many other occasions calling for you to address an individual or a group, formally or informally, in your chair or on your feet, with or without prior notice and time for preparation, and with or without audiovisual aids and other presentation support. This may be over lunch or during a private meeting, but it may also be an occasion on which you must deliver a report of some kind to management, shareholders, clients, fellow members of trade or professional associations, or even to peers, business or professional associates, and visitors.

That is not all. You may be called upon to present an award, to introduce another speaker, or to make an announcement. Moreover, as other executives and professionals often do, you may belong to the in-house speaker's bureau that many large organizations maintain. Such facilities support the organizations's pubic relations department by being available at no charge to provide a guest speaker for meetings and seminars, gaining publicity and enhancing the organization's image. In many organizations, every senior member of the staff is expected to be available for this service.

It is common, therefore, for executives and staff professionals alike to be called on to prepare, organize, and deliver seminars and other training sessions, often as in-house activities.

Unfortunately, a great many people are all but paralyzed at the prospect of speaking before a group—what is commonly known as "stage fright," or "platform paralysis." This is a serious concern, one surrounded by excessive mythology. Those myths will be addressed in these pages, and dissipated. If you have that all-too-common fear of facing an audience, there is help here for you.

Despite the inevitable main focus on the individual standing on the dais and delivering the meat of the preparation, use of "media" cannot be neglected. The artful and effective use of the various media—posters, overhead projectors, slides, filmstrips, and other audiovisual aids—is an essential element of all but the most informal presentations. Methods for creating, using, and taking fullest possible advantage of such aids will be explained. Further, the use of today's desktop computers and desktop publishing software will be discussed and explained, as the subjects pertain to the creation of and aids to presentations.

Also, the subject of sales persuasion will be discussed. A presentation is always a sales argument, for you are inevitably trying to sell something to your listeners, whether it is merchandise or an idea. Any presentation, even one that is highly polished and flawless in a technical sense, fails if it does not sell. And selling is never an accident; it happens only by careful design and intent.

To bring that result about—to sell your arguments and expositions to your audience—you must be credible: Your audience must perceive you as an expert, as knowing what you are talking about. In the beginning, before you appear on the platform and begin to speak, you audience normally accepts you as an expert and an authority. The mere fact that you appear before them is the evidence. Thus, success does not require that you prove this as much as it does that you avoid disproving it.

HERMAN HOLTZ

Contents

Introduction

DEFINING PRESENTATION

A popular assumption is that the word *presentation* refers always to a formal speech or lecture. Most of what is written about the subject unfortunately supports that narrow notion.

When I surveyed the extant literature on the subject, I found that much of it adhered to that popular notion: Many books treat the word *presentation* as virtually synonymous with *public speaking*, stressing that latter subject. On the other hand, many others who write or lecture on public speaking, education, training, selling, writing, marketing, and other related subjects also use the word presentation freely, but each with a different spin. It is probably inevitable that everyone interprets the word in terms of his or her own direct interest and major career field. Show business personality and former salesman Ed McMahon sees it as part of both selling and show business, while professional speaker/trainer/author/consultant Nido Qubein sees it as communication.

An advertisement that appeared in *Computer Shopper* bears the headline INSTANT PRESENTATIONS, $44.95. What does it really mean? Advertisers of computer software designed for graphics and desktop publishing focus on the visual aspects of presentations, as do sellers of supplies for creating slides, posters, flip charts, transparencies for overhead projectors, and other graphic aids. Visit the makers of films and videotapes and you get still another view: You find you attention focused on cameras, lighting, props, and performers with professionally smooth speaking voices and mannerisms, plus all the magic that can be produced on a screen via these media. And not too surprisingly, professional writers tend to see many of the things they write—for example, reports, proposals, scripts, and even résumés—as presentations. Those in sales and marketing often refer to their presentations—usually elaborate sales presentations, with a staff of several presenters, armed with scripts, posters, flip charts, and other such aids—as dog-and-pony shows. Business executives and public officials think of speeches as presentations. At banquets, a presenter or master of ceremonies introduces other speakers, may make an award to a featured guest, and otherwise is a kind of "utility" man or woman at an occasion that consists largely of making a number of presentations.

The subject of presentations covers all these things and more. Presentations may be formal, semi-formal, or informal; they may be entirely verbal, entirely in media (that is, in printed, audio, or visual media form), or any combination of these. The purpose is to entertain, inform, orient, indoctrinate, and/or persuade.

WHO MAKES PRESENTATIONS?

Presentations are made by people in all walks of life and on all sorts of occasions. Teachers, lecturers, professional speakers, and salespeople, among many others, make presentations as a routine part of their daily work. Public officials, politicians, business executives, professionals, members and officers of associations, radio and TV announcers, entertainers, demagogues, and sundry others make presentations frequently, if not daily. Many others make presentations occasionally, as a business or social requirement.

The majority of presentations are elements of sales and marketing. By this I mean marketing in the larger sense, as something we all do: We *all* sell or try to sell ideas every day, even many times a day. Arguing for a favored restaurant for dinner is an exercise in marketing. Professional communications consultants Karen Berg and Andrew Gilman say early in their book, *Get to the Point*, that the word *presentation* includes "short and informal talks with clearly defined objectives that take place most often in a work-related context." When a presenter utters laudatory remarks as a preliminary to honoring a guest, he or she is making a presentation— marketing, working hard to "sell," to persuade everyone of the worth of the honoree. The politician works to persuade listeners that voting for him or her is in the listener's own best interest. The Chairman of the Board addressing the shareholders at an annual meeting is explaining the worth of the corporation and its programs, telling them what they came to hear. Teachers are making a presentation of valuable knowledge and perhaps even precious wisdom to students. Presentations are made to indoctrinate employees, defend actions, explain programs, solicit followers, promote causes, present papers, and otherwise furnish information, and views of all kinds and on all occasions, but always to sell an idea or an action, to literally *present* listeners with something of value.

Thus, a presentation is a focused address, with a clear-cut purpose, and so involves both marketing and selling something. This requires identifying and satisfying needs or wants. Beer is sold by TV presentations that show us how beer satisfies our need for entertainment and good times. Lee Iaccoca made a powerful sales presentation to the American public and our government, persuading us that it was for our own good (it satisfied one of our needs) that we lend Chrysler Corporation enough money to keep them in business and save the jobs of all the Chrysler workers. Sales are made by demonstrating to the buyers how the sale satisfies *their* needs. In the sense that an audience views, hears, or reads a presentation seeking satisfaction of a want or need, *every* presentation worthy of the name is a marketing or sales presentation.

Each writer on the subject of presentation offers his or her own definition of a presentation. However, all the authors, including the one you're reading now, agree on certain details:

- Have a clear and specific objective: You must know what it is that you wish to persuade your audience to believe, accept, do, or decide.

- Plan the presentation carefully and prepare for it, organizing your material logically with a proper opening, middle, and close.

- Perfect your platform manner and be thoroughly professional as a presenter in all respects.

- Be ready—thoroughly rehearsed and thoroughly expert—in what you are presenting.

- Let the audience in on your main objective or main point, and do it early.

- Don't waste the time of your audience rambling or going off on tangents; be efficient in delivering your material.

Obviously, some of these exhortations cannot be applied literally when you must make informal and impromptu presentations. However, if you have mastered the skills needed to make a thoroughly professional formal presentation, you should have little difficulty in making a quite acceptable informal and impromptu one.

In the discussions and presentations (yes, presentations) that follow, the major emphasis will be on verbal skills—standing up and speaking to individuals and groups, large and small. In addition, the essential principles of organizing and delivering specific information addressing a specific objective will be highlighted. The role of presentation aids and alternative forms of presentation, primarily the written presentation, will not be neglected; it is a most important role, and can make or break a presentation.

This book is intended for the executive, professional, official, or other individual who may be called upon to make a presentation of any kind—formal or informal, planned or impromptu, oral or written, to superiors or subordinates, to peers or associates, to friends or strangers, on any occasion, and on any subject.

With that rather tall order, we better get started!

1

Presentations: Some Basic Information

The word presentation is a most general term that probably has too many meanings to begin with, but is a most important part of the business world, the professional world, and the world in general.

THE AUDIENCE ALWAYS COMES FIRST

A presentation requires both a presenter and an audience. Strictly speaking, a single person can constitute an audience, and a presentation can be a simple, informal explanation. Almost any discussion can be a presentation. The kinds of presentations and the basic principles of a good presentation have nothing to do with the size of the audience or with formality or the lack of it. Before we tackle the rather difficult task of identifying the many kinds of presentation, we will first review the principles of a good presentation.

Remember that persuasion is always a general objective for a presentation, but in addition, there is a requirement to have a distinct objective, which you make known to your listeners in opening your presentation. That is your commitment to your audience. Concentrate on delivering what you promised; that is, get to the point without undue delay. Think and speak in terms of *me* and *you* (*you* being the members of the audience and *me* being you, the presenter). Your needs and wants, usually for approval and ego gratification, are second in importance. But they will be gratified, if you please the audience. You can count on it. In this, as in other things, getting what you want depends on giving the other individual what he or she wants. Remember at all times that the audience, not you, is the reason for the presentation. You are on the platform to do something for those people seated before you, and they owe you nothing unless you earn it. If you get their approval—smiles, applause, congratulations or other manifestations—it is because you have earned it. They don't applaud merely to be polite, either: That kind of applause is truly faint praise. An audience is quick to respond with applause and even standing ovations when they are pleased with what you have delivered to them. Audiences are not naturally hostile; they want you to succeed—to be interesting and deliver what they came to hear. They might be apprehensive, however, fearing that you will be a deadly bore, and hopeful that they will gain enough useful or entertaining information to be worth the ordeal. They may be pleasantly surprised when your presentation is interesting, and most grateful when it is pleasurable. They show their gratitude with enthusiastic endorsement through smiles, applause, and approaching you at the end of the session with handshakes and personal thank-yous.

Bear in mind that the audience has come to gain something. They have come to gain certain information or diversion they want and believe they have been promised. They are willing to pay with their time, as the minimum. They have agreed to give up their time to sit through a presentation with the expectation of getting what they want. Of course, there are many other occasions, such as formal seminars, where the attendees have paid in their time and in hard cash also, often traveling some distance to hear what you have to say. (One of the most devastating remarks I have ever read on a post-seminar evaluation form was, "Where do I apply for a refund?" That was a long time ago, but I hope to never read one like that again.)

WHAT DOES THE AUDIENCE WANT?

In some cases, an audience has come to sit and be entertained, and that may even be implicit in the original announcement. Usually some clue as to the nature of the presentation is furnished by whomever has sponsored it. Some business organizations have regularly scheduled dinner meetings at which an after-dinner speaker is a regular feature. The speaker at these events is usually invited to speak on a business or professional topic of interest, rather than merely to entertain, although there are exceptions to this. At conventions, for example, there are usually many speeches and seminars conducted on strictly business or professional subjects, while a professional comedian may have been retained to entertain the attendees after lunch or dinner. Some comedians work regularly as after-dinner speakers at such affairs. Their presentations are comedy routines, played strictly for laughs. (I have more than once seen Henny Youngman, the acknowledged master of the one-liner joke, in that role, for example. Screen comedienne, Bette Midler, did part of her apprenticeship speaking and entertaining student associations at many universities.) The audience has come to be entertained, in such situations; that is what they expect and that is the basis on which they will judge the quality of the presentation.

On the other hand, the organization may make it a policy to arrange after-dinner presentations by some expert on topics of direct interest to members of the audience. The local retail business owner's club, for example, might invite a speaker to offer his or her views on retail marketing or on some special aspect of retail marketing. In this case, the audience has come in the hope of learning something that will contribute to the success of their businesses or their careers in the business world. But even then, an audience is composed of individuals, and their specific hopes for information are likely to vary accordingly. For example, some members of the audience may be highly experienced retailers who know that what they hear from the speaker may or may not be new and appropriate information for them. However, they are willing to gamble and invest their time and perhaps some of their dollars in the hope of learning something new and useful. Others may be less experienced and eager to hear anything a more experienced retailer or recognized expert authority has to say, while still others may have some specific problems or questions and hope that the speaker will cover them or that they will get a chance to ask some specific questions about their most immediate concerns.

On one recent occasion, I was asked to speak to a group at a luncheon meeting on marketing by mail. It is important to know as much as possible about your audience in advance of speaking to them. I had accordingly ascertained that they were all in some aspect of public relations and had only limited knowledge of or experience in marketing by mail. I knew that, faced with an audience not knowledgeable in mail order or direct mail, I could not really cover enough of that complex subject in the 15 or 20 minutes allotted me to be very useful. Therefore, I merely introduced the subject in a very few minutes and then invited questions from attendees. That resulted in a lively half-hour, almost surely a better one than I would have otherwise achieved. The ability to respond spontaneously to questions asked at random is a valuable asset for a presenter: Audiences do appreciate being able to ask questions when they get sensible answers. Work at developing that skill for those occasions when it is appropriate to invite questions from your audience, but you must be quite expert in your subject and able to respond spontaneously. It would be a suicidal strategy if you were not able to do so.

KNOWING WHAT TO EXPECT

Attendees at a presentation have some basis for expecting some specific information. Their expectations may be based on any of several different possibilities. If the name of the presenter is sufficiently well known—Bob Hope, for example—the audience may easily infer from that alone what to expect—a comedy routine, in this case. If the name of the speaker is Lee Iaccoca, they are less sure, however. It is almost certain that it will be Lee Iaccoca's views on business, economics, or government, and might or might not also be entertaining in that context. In any case, it will not be a comedy routine, whether it does or does not include a few jokes. If the guest is Mark Russell, attendees may expect an original routine of political satire, accompanied by satirical ditties written and performed by Russell.

If the occasion is a seminar, there has almost surely been a descriptive brochure circulated, announcing it, with the inclusion of an outline of content and highlights of the specific information promised.

The identity of the organization and nature of the occasion may be enough to indicate what the subject will be. If it is an awards dinner, attendees will expect presentations about the organization and the honoree, whose name would have been announced in advance. If it is a trade association to which you belong, those seated in the room expect something concerning your industry. In most cases, however, the audience will know the title of the address or seminar and may even have some descriptive literature included in the announcement.

There are occasions when an audience has no idea in advance of the occasion that there will even be a presentation, much less knowledge of the subject of the presentation. They may be suddenly summoned to a meeting at work, for example, with no advance notice. (And you may have been assigned the job of making the presentation with no advance notice!) In that case, the audience expects you, as the presenter, to give them an idea of what the presentation is about, as a first order of business. In your opening remarks, you ought to be as clear as possible in telling them what to expect, even when there has been a prior announcement and descriptive matter furnished. If, for example, you are explaining the new group insurance plan to employees, let them know immediately that a new insurance plan is being adopted, and that you are about to explain the plan.

In more formal situations, such as giving a seminar that has been announced weeks in advance, the brochure that has been designed to encourage attendance may not be quite as descriptive of the main objective as it ought to be. For example, in presenting a seminar I give on proposal writing, I have found it most helpful to open by explaining that while the seminar's title promises useful guidance in proposal writing, the real objective (what some might call the hidden agenda) is not really proposal writing at all but winning contracts. That is, proposal writing is the means, but winning contracts is the goal. That tells the attendees immediately what the session is really all about, what to expect—information on how to win contracts—and thus how to judge the merit of the presentation, as well as what information tidbits to be especially watchful for. An all-day seminar is usually a series of presentations, each on a major topic, often by more than one presenter, and each should be so introduced by the presenter.

A *SUCCESSFUL* PRESENTATION

Whether your presentation is a success or not depends primarily on one thing: whether the audience believes that they got what they came for; that is, whether the audience is *satisfied* that they got what they came for. But just what does that mean? Does everyone in the audience at a variety show love the performance of each star and superstar—for example, Bob Hope presenting awards at some TV awards gala? Obviously not; not even a superstar is perfect. (I cannot stand some shows and performers my wife dearly loves, and the reverse is also true.) Superstars please the vast majority of their audiences. That applies to any presentation, even those made by you and me. It is more than likely—it is almost certain—that some members of an audience will not be satisfied with your presentation, and the reasons may be highly individual ones. (I have had at least one attendee recording his remarks in the post-session evaluation sheet concentrate on criticizing my clothing, urging me to seek out a fashion consultant!) But if most of the attendees approves of a presentation, it is a success. Majority opinion is all we have to judge by and all we can count on.

Note that this definition of success made no stipulations as to how eloquent or entertaining you were, to your sartorial elegance, to how smooth and polished your platform manner was, to how effectively you used presentation aids, nor to the contribution of any other peripheral and ancillary elements. It stipulated only that a majority of the attendees were satisfied that they got what they came for. That is a practical minimum as a standard.

The reverse is also true. Suppose you are an eloquent speaker, you make a highly entertaining presentation, dress impeccably, have a marvelous presence, and use numerous visual aids, but fail to furnish the information the audience came to hear and thus fail to *satisfy* the audience. Could you call that a successful presentation? Of course not. Keeping your bargain with your audience and delivering what you promised, whether it was by specific promise or by implication, is the first requirement. When an attendee says "I picked up twelve pointers, including how to appear to be the low bidder," he is saying that he got what he came for. When the vice-president of a large company refers to one item covered by a presenter in an all-day seminar and says, "That one tip alone was worth the entire day," the presentation was a great success, as far as he was concerned. There is really no middle ground in this: There are only satisfied and dissatisfied audiences, even if there are many degrees of satisfaction and dissatisfaction.

IS OFFERING THE RIGHT INFORMATION ENOUGH?

None of this is to say that simply offering the right information is all there is to success in presentation. If your presentation is bad enough, you may offer the information you promised but fail entirely to deliver it.

"Eh? How's that?" you say immediately. "How can I fail to deliver the information when I state it plainly in front of an audience? If they don't get what I laid out for them it isn't my fault, is it?"

Yes, it is your fault when your audience doesn't get the information you offer. You are responsible for the delivery. If you succeed in boring your audience enough with a lackluster, slumber-inducing presentation, you may be almost certain that they will not get the pertinent information when you finally drop it before them. If you speak entirely in obscure jargon or in "75-cent words," many will not understand your message. If you mumble or speak too softly to be heard in the far rows, you won't get much across. Even if you are a talented speaker and your presentation is extremely well done, you can't lay all the blame on the audience for failures to communicate. It is your responsibility as a presenter to see to it that your audience gets the information—recognizes and understands it, that is. You are responsible for *knowing* and *understanding* your audience, and so judging accurately what is necessary to achieve true communication. You are responsible for verifying that you are coming across: It is easy enough to recognize when bright, attentive eyes are hanging on to your words and gestures, or when those eyes are staring dully at you with the obvious yearning to have you end their ordeal.

THE KINDS OF PRESENTATIONS

There are many kinds of presentations you might be called upon to make, and they vary or can be classified in more than one way. We will discuss length and purpose of classification criteria.

Length

Presentations vary in length from a few minutes to several days. For example, you may be a sales professional, retailing a relatively inexpensive item—perhaps cosmetics or shoes. That would normally call for a brief presentation, usually delivered to individuals. On the other hand, if you are selling automobiles or houses, your presentation is likely to be a great deal longer, delivered frequently to couples. (Selling big-tag items, such as houses and automobiles, is not a "one-call business," which means you must usually make a series of presentations to win over a prospect.) Or you may be an after dinner speaker, making a few remarks and allotted 15 or 20 minutes to do so. You may be making full-blown speeches of an hour or more. But it is also possible that you may be delivering an all-day seminar or even one that runs to several days.

Purpose

Sales Presentations

A large part of all presentations made, especially (but not exclusively) oral ones made face-to-face, are sales presentations, made for no other purpose than to close sales as a direct result of the presentation. Aside from the impromptu one-on-one sales presentation across a retail counter or on the selling floor, there are formal, full-dress sales presentations. There was yet-to-be-entertainment-star Ed McMahon selling potato slicers to a crowd he managed to gather to witness his demonstration and hear his persuasive words. There is the itinerant sales professional calling on department stores, manufacturers, and other mass buyers making informal presentations to buyers, department heads, purchasing agents, and even to proprietors of smaller establishments. There is the door-to-door seller of brushes, cosmetics, and encyclopedias, making presentations to individual householders and couples. There is the party-seller, making presentations to small groups in people's homes. There is the auctioneer addressing a crowd gathered to find bargains and be entertained at the same time. There is the presenter seeking to close a large contract by formal presentation—that traditional "dog-and-pony show" mentioned earlier, with its array of visual and audiovisual aids and often with one or more assistants—to a staff of senior people in the customer's board room. There is the formal sales presentation disguised and announced as a free public seminar held in a large meeting room and lasting for at least an hour and sometimes even longer. And no doubt there are many other sales presentations that I have not covered here.

Other Purposes

Aside from sales, there are many presentations made for other reasons and purposes. A convention usually opens with a "keynote address," for example. This is supposed to introduce the convention to the gathered attendees. The keynote speaker will usually speak at some length—perhaps an hour—and will welcome the attendees, introduce this year's convention, present the philosophy of the gathering, perhaps review the prior year's convention and the year since, and introduce another speaker, probably one of several. However, in a truly formal setting, there will have been a prior presentation of a few minutes by some official of the organization who will have introduced the keynote speaker and who will reappear to introduce each succeeding speaker.

A symposium bears some superficial resemblance to a convention in that it is a gathering of individuals with some related interest who gather to discuss one or more major topics relating to that mutual interest. Those with interests in the space programs of NASA, for example, have held symposia to present professional papers and exchange information for the purpose of furthering the advancement of the science and industry of space programs. This aspect—delivering formal papers to be subsequently published as the *Proceedings*—is also true of many conventions, especially those held by professional societies.

Conventions often include a variety of seminars in addition to the main event. These are generally held to impart specialized information of one sort or another. *Training* magazine, for example, holds an annual convention at the New York

Hilton, at which a series of half-day (three-hour) seminars are offered, each on some subject of interest to those in the training field.

At many conventions, there are other kinds of sideshows: There are hospitality suites and other special sessions offered by sellers in private rooms, at which prospects are offered refreshments of some sort and invited to hear the sellers' special sales presentations.

I have referred already to after-dinner speakers, to awards presentations, and to similar events. These make up a great portion of all presentations.

Many presentations, made for public relations purposes, are an indirect form of selling and sales promotion. You might use any kind of forum for this—seminars, either your own or as a guest speaker at others' seminars; radio and TV appearances as a guest on appropriate programs; luncheon and dinner meetings; meetings of clubs and other organizations; as one of the several varieties of convention sideshows described here; and/or on any other occasion where you can address an audience and promote whatever it is you are to promote.

Another purpose for which many presentations are made is the political purpose—to be elected or to gain support for favored legislation. The presenter in this case may be a professional politician, a volunteer supporting a cause in which he or she believes, a student running for office in high school or college, or a member of an association running for office in the organization.

Finally, there are the professional speakers, those who speak for fees. In this case, the purpose of the presentation may vary greatly, but the purpose of the presenter is the same in each case: He or she makes presentations for money, for income. Many speak for fees on a full-time basis, while many do so on a part-time basis or as one element of full-time self-employment. For example, many professional writers and consultants also speak for fees. On the other hand, many professional speakers—those who identify themselves as speakers primarily—also write and consult. The three professions—speaking, writing, and consulting—complement each other.

WHERE MIGHT YOU BE
CALLED UPON TO SPEAK?

You might be asked to make a presentation anywhere: the public sales stand, such as Ed McMahon used on the Atlantic City boardwalk many years ago; the public auction; the awards dinner; the convention hall; the hotel ballroom; and other such sites. If you are an educator, you will be called upon to address students in a class, but you might also be asked to speak to parents, teachers, or peers. If you are a professional speaker, you might also be called upon to address students in colleges and universities; they are popular markets for professional speakers. You might also be called upon to speak on cruise ships, in halls, in auditoriums, at private banquets, at conventions, and at almost any location.

It is not at all unlikely that you will be called upon at least occasionally to speak, informally and without prior notice, to an individual or group of employees, associates, customers, or others with some specific objective to inform, argue, or persuade. You may be called upon, at a small luncheon with a group, to rise to your feet for a few remarks. Or you may be a retail salesperson selling consumer goods to customers across the counter. Those, too, are presentations.

The principles of making such informal presentations are not truly different from those of making the more formal ones. Inevitably, I will be forced to discuss the subject more in terms of the more or less formal speaking situations than of the impromptu and informal ones. That is not intended to discount the importance of the latter; mastery of presentations of all kinds is important.

WHAT KINDS OF PEOPLE
BECOME PRESENTERS?

Almost anyone may be called upon to make presentations of almost any kind, and a great many of us must often make the kind of informal presentations just described.

Professionals

Professionals and paraprofessionals of all kinds are quite likely to be called upon to speak on numerous occasions. The list of such people includes physicians, dentists, lawyers, architects, engineers, chemists, certified public accountants, physicists, pharmacists, psychologists, writers, consultants, technicians, nurses, instructors, computer programmers, systems analysts, designers, and other specialists. In many cases, such specialists are asked to make presentations in connection with the associations and societies to which they belong and also, in certain cases, in support of sales presentations organized by others, for example, the sales manager or director of marketing in their organizations. Or they may be designated members of the organization's internal speaker's bureau who are assigned to speak to any group requesting a speaker.

Executives

Business executives of all kinds and at all levels within their organizations are quite likely to be asked to address groups of various kinds, both within and without their companies and the other organizations to which they belong. In many cases, the executive is also a professional or paraprofessional, and thus may be called upon in either role. In all cases, the executive, like the professional, may be a member of the organization's speaker's bureau.

Elected Politicians and Public Speakers

Almost anyone might be a politician on a temporary or transient basis, and those who are full-time professional politicians are too well-known to all of us to need further comment or description. The same may be said for professional speakers. Note that both speak for fees. Speaking fees are a major income source for a great many elected officials, especially those in Congress.

Public Official

Many public officials are politicians, having won their positions via elections. That is not the case with all: Many public officials are appointed to office. Many speak for fees, but many others will speak as a public service, without a fee. Public officials, as a group, are called upon frequently and expected to be able to speak publicly.

Before going further into the subject of public speaking, let's take a look at another form of presentation, the written form. That is the subject of the next chapter.

2

Written Presentations

Making a presentation, whether vocal or visual, is a communications art. While the skills required to communicate effectively for each form and medium are similar, they are at the same time different, and each has its own pros and cons.

Any serious discussion on the main subject, presentations, must give at least some time to the written form of the art. Most effective presenters have far greater enthusiasm for and pride in the public speaking aspects than the writing aspects of presentations. Both fear and reluctance may be at work here. Many people have a fear of public speaking and that accounts for their reluctance to speak to an audience. On the other hand, many people dislike writing, and it is their *dislike* of what they *perceive* to be an onerous chore, not fear, that accounts for their reluctance to write. It requires a degree of courage to become a public speaker, especially to learn to be completely at ease on the platform. One may justifiably take great pride in having summoned up the courage to learn how to be an effective public speaker.

It is important to learn how to write as well as to speak if you are to be an effective presenter. As a marketer for myself, for clients, and for past employers, I have written many sales presentations of various kinds.

As a frequent presenter of seminars on proposal writing, I have always taken pains early in the session to impress audiences with the truth that a proposal is most definitely a sales presentation. It can't very well be anything else when its entire purpose for existence is to make a sale.

WRITTEN PRESENTATIONS

Verbal presentations are abundantly in evidence around us every day. But written presentations also confront us every day. Even if you happen to be someone who attends a great many lectures, seminars, banquets, conventions, and other such occasions, you probably are exposed to at least as many written presentations as vocal ones. Let's have a look at your morning mail alone, for example, and see what we can find there:

1. Here is one of those six-panel, $8\frac{1}{2} \times 11$-inch folders describing a seminar on some subject—perhaps computer programming or modernizing your office procedures—and urging you to register immediately and without fail if you wish to guarantee your seat at this upcoming session and reap the benefits of this outstanding program.

2. Here is a salesletter from the department store who sold you a TV last year, advising you of a tremendous special sale and pleading with you to come in early to take advantage of it and beat the crowd to all the marvelous bargains.

3. A thick catalog from a mail order house is in your mailbox today. It is loaded with beautiful and expensive color photos of costly furs and other clothing, with lengthy explanations and sales appeals for each, including an offer of easy payments and all major credit cards accepted.

4. A letter from a candidate for public office presents her campaign pledges and promises and appeals to

you for both a donation to her campaign and your vote on election day.

5. An envelope covered with sales messages on the outside is stuffed with sales literature, you find, including a salesletter, a brochure, an order form, and a postage-paid return envelope, the obligatory minimum ensemble for a proper direct-mail package.

6. Another envelope produces a letter and brochure appealing for donations for homeless and starving children in some far-off place, with many photos and an explanation of how little money is required of you to help support one of these unfortunate children.

7. There is a note and business card left by a real estate salesman who wants to sell your home for you. It's a brief enough presentation, but a presentation it is. Call him and you will be treated to a much expanded vocal presentation.

8. A business card from an automobile salesman, with a note scrawled on it, offers to give you a great trade-in on the automobile in your driveway. As a presentation it's quite similar to that of the real estate salesman, and he will be equally eloquent in a face-to-face presentation, should you respond.

9. You find an envelope stuffed with coupons, and a little brochure advising you that you are invited to use all of these and save a great deal of money.

10. Finally, there is a mimeographed letter from the local Neighborhood Watch group, urging you to come to their next meeting and explaining the importance of what the group does.

Multiply these few examples by all the business days of the year and you get a brief idea of the written presentations that you are likely to see as an ordinary citizen and householder. But let us go to your office and see that number of written presentations multiplied even further. Written appeals—proposals, brochures, letters, circulars, posters, and signs—besiege you all day. The new luncheonette around the corner wants you to try their carry out and free delivery services. The local copy shop appeals to you with a circular distributed in your building. A nearby printer sends you information about seasonal specials now available. An office supplies emporium and an art supplies store send you catalogs and forms to apply for a line of credit. An express shipping service sends you literature announcing a new courier service. Several proposals arrive on your desk. An office designer sends you expensive literature illustrating her work and soliciting your account. Reports from three of your sales representatives arrive at your desk. The morning mail includes more than a dozen résumés resulting from your help-wanted advertising.

That isn't the end of it. You have your own written presentations to create. Several customers have written with questions about your products, and you must dictate correspondence answering their questions and trying to convert the inquiries into orders. You also must prepare a report for a meeting to take place later in the week where you will be expected to bring the staff up to date on your projects. You will also be expected to make your contribution to the corporation's annual report, due soon.

Let us also not overlook the fact that every presentation, even a verbal one delivered from a platform, begins life as something in writing. This is especially true for those presentations that are prepared before the camera for big- or small-screen use—as movie films or videotapes—which are almost always based on a carefully designed shooting script written by specialists in scripting. Every effective presenter has first planned the presentation on paper. Few experienced speakers memorize a script because it rarely makes for a truly effective presentation, but they do lay out their presentations in written form and follow the written form generally.

The truth of that became quite apparent when, along with another individual acting as interviewer, I undertook to make an audiotape version of one of my books, reading from a prepared script. After hours of "takes" and "retakes," it became apparent that reading from the script before us was not going to work. It all came out sounding quite mechanical and lifeless; it lacked the spark of spontaneity. Finally, we abandoned the script and conducted a dialogue along the general lines of the script, but without reading from it. The tape began to come to life, and we succeeded in creating an interesting and credible presentation.

In a great many cases where the primary medium of presentation is the speaker on the dais, listeners are also given written material—manuals, brochures, or other handouts—to supplement the verbal presentation and provide something for subsequent review. So even verbal presentations are not always purely vocal ones.

SIMILARITIES AND DIFFERENCES

Verbal and written presentations have many similarities and they have many differences. Some presentations, both verbal and written, are made purely for entertainment, and they are successful or unsuccessful on the basis of how well they succeed in being entertaining. Others have the common purpose of conveying information effectively, and that means persuading the audience—listeners and readers—to accept or believe what is being offered. That is as true for a how-to seminar or manual as it is for a pure and unabashed sales pitch. When I urge attendees at my seminars and readers of my books to start their consulting practices on a modest basis and in their own homes, I don't ask them to do so merely because I say it is the best way to do it; I employ logical argument and case histories to convince them that my advice is based soundly on reason and experience, that what I recommend will work for them. When I suggest that a free newsletter is an effective public relations device, I not only explain why I believe this but I go into detail in explaining how to create and use a free newsletter effectively. When a maintenance manual prescribes a preventive or corrective procedure, it ought to also   .

indicate the purpose and wisdom of the procedure, if the reader is expected to take the recommendation seriously. This is true whether the advice is delivered in writing, in a classroom, or in an auditorium. However, the function must dictate the form—the medium, in this case—and we will see how this works in typical cases.

FUNCTION VERSUS FORM

Dave Yoho is a successful professional speaker, with a marvelous voice and a most effective delivery. But he developed that wonderful voice in overcoming severe speech impediments as a child. It is an inspiring story, and he relates it to illustrate what the human spirit can accomplish. Obviously, this story is far more effective when related by Yoho from the dais than it is when described in print because listeners can hear this golden voice, while readers can only imagine it. That points up one major difference between the two media, but only one; there are others, for each medium offers its own peculiar characteristics, which can be advantages or disadvantages for any given case. There are situations in which the verbal presentation is the most effective or most practical way to deliver the message, but the reverse is also true: In some cases, the written presentation is advantageous, and in some it is a must. Let's look at a few examples illustrating this and comparing the written presentation with the verbal one.

The Proposal Form

Proposals are almost always made in written format (although they may be followed up subsequently with a verbal presentation and are sometimes supplemented with slides or audiotapes). A procurement that is of great size, importance, and/or complexity is usually one that the requestor must study, and possibly needs also to confer on with associates before making a decision. Spoken words are transient and do not lend themselves to extended study and evaluation; only a written presentation is truly suitable for that.

There is another compelling reason for proposals to be written. In many cases, such as in large engineering projects, the proposal must include a thick package of drawings, charts, graphs, specifications, and other detailed data that could not be handled effectively in a verbal delivery.

There is yet another important reason: Proposals and many other written presentations must serve as convenient references, and only the printed form is truly suitable for that. In fact, in one case, where a three-volume proposal was developed to compete for a major government training project, the proposal had to serve as the operating manual for several months after the proposer won the contract.

Annual Reports

Publicly held corporations produce annual reports for their shareholders and for others, such as bankers, customers, and prospective customers. The main purpose is to present required financial data and certified by a firm of certified public accountants, but there is some other explanatory data included. It usually concerns the major events of the year, such as achievements in sales, acquisitions, divestitures, and problems solved, and a projection of plans for the year to come. To a large degree, the typical annual report is also a sales presentation, portraying the corporation in the best light possible for the reassurance and gratification of investors and others who have an interest in the organization.

Some of these annual reports, particularly those emanating from small corporations, are quite simple "plain vanilla" documents, strictly business and dealing with stark facts only. Others, coming from major corporations, are quite extensive and expensive, with full-color illustrations, elaborate typesetting, printing on costly paper, and with other such refinements.

Aside from legal requirements to make such reports, corporations use these reports as public relations tools to enhance their public images. They have these reports printed in large quantities, making a mass mailing to shareholders and others and distributing them further throughout the year. Only a printed presentation is practical for such distribution. Where the presentation must reach a great many individuals over a wide area, the printed presentation is usually the only one that works well.

Finally, as in the case of proposals, annual reports are publications many users keep, at least until the next year's annual report, as more or less permanent references.

Direct Mail

Reference was made earlier to the typical direct-mail package and its minimum elements, which include a salesletter, brochure, order form, and return envelope. That does not mean that all direct-mail packages follow this pattern rigorously. Many do not include a return envelope, and a great many include more than one brochure and several other elements. Some are mailed in plain white envelopes, while others are mailed in envelopes covered on the outside with "teaser copy." These are only two variants of the basic model; there are many more, limited only by the imagination of the entrepreneurs and experts in direct mail. Whatever the pattern and number of elements, however, the package is a presentation or series of presentations, depending on how you wish to regard it. Even the order form bears a brief presentation of its own: No true direct marketer misses an opportunity to add to the sales messages.

Traditionally, the salesletter is the central element of a direct mail package, on the assumption that the recipient will read the letter first. It presents the basic appeal, explains the proposition generally, and sets the tone for the entire package. The other elements stem directly from it and support the arguments. There may be just one brochure in the package, offering some elaboration on the material presented by the salesletter, or there may be several brochures, each devoted to expanding a single element or argument of the presentation. (There is a direct mail platitude that says, "The more you tell, the more you sell," and many mailers believe that several brochures greatly strengthen the impact of a package.) In any case, a direct mail package is a sales presentation to be sent out to many thousands of prospects all over the country. Again, a written and printed presentation is by far the most practical approach in most cases.

Targeted Audiences

The arguments so far offered for written presentations have been based on such considerations as the sheer size of the audience, the amount and nature of detail required, and the need to have the presentation in a form that constitutes a more or less permanent reference. There is also the consideration of targeted audiences. Take the case of the direct mail package, for example. If the desired audience, the prospects to whom the sales appeal is to be presented, is the general public, perhaps a verbal presentation made via radio or TV would be adequate. Most such presentations are directed to the general public. They would have to be, for there are not many ways to target an audience of broadcast listeners and watchers. They can be targeted only by whatever listening/viewing habits they may have, such as those who listen to and watch daytime programs versus those who listen to and watch evening programs and those who listen to and watch late-night programs.

You can target your audience geographically, although only in broad terms, by deciding which radio and TV stations to use. The only other way to target broadcast audiences is by type of program. Daytime soap operas and talk shows are watched by women primarily, whereas weekend sports programs attract men more than women. However, if you wished to target attorneys or construction workers, you would not be able to do so very effectively with broadcast media. (The sole exception would be to advertise during a highly specialized program, but even that is not very dependable for close targeting.) But you can target people by many specific demographic elements with direct mail because you can rent mailing lists by occupation, by zip codes, by economic status, by whether they rent or own their homes, by buying history and habits, and by many other characteristics that can make a large difference in the response you get to your presentations. Therefore, if you wish to target your audience with any great degree of precision, you must turn to direct mail. (There is telemarketing, selling via telephone communication, which can be used to reach a targeted audience, but it is far from being as popular or as easy to use as direct mail.)

Advantages of Verbal Presentations

The cases we have just discussed are cases where the required functions dictated that verbal presentations were not suitable and written presentations were required to get the job done. But there are cases where something that is inherent in the nature of the medium dictates which is best to use. The case of professional speaker Dave Yoho was one in which the nature of vocal presentation offers an advantage that cannot be matched by a written presentation—that is, Yoho's fine speaking voice demonstrated for itself the dramatic results of a youngster's determination to overcome his handicap. If you were to read the material used by such outstanding performers as Bob Hope or George Burns, instead of watching and listening to them, you would probably not find the material entertaining at all. That would be immeasurably true in the case of the late comedian Jack Benny, whose gestures, grimaces, intonations, and, especially, his timing were even more essential parts of his performance than were his lines.

This is also true of presentations from the dais. A large part of your success—the success of all good speakers on the platform, regardless of the subject—is due to these same factors. (We will discuss these in far more detail a bit later.)

However, although, as the platform personality, you have these great advantages—and used well, they are indeed great advantages—there are some inherent traits in written presentations that offer advantages over the verbal medium. Let's consider a few of these.

Permanence

The permanence of words on a page has a functional advantage most clearly illustrated by presentations to be used as records or reference documents. However, that permanence has another advantage: After listening to you speak, the listener cannot recall the words spoken very well, other than by asking you to repeat what you said. That is not usually very easy to do. With a written presentation, however, the reader can reread and study the words as many times as he or she wishes.

That characteristic offers an advantage to you as the presenter (i.e., as the writer) too. As a speaker, you hope that you communicated effectively with your audience, and you can use certain techniques to ensure that. However, as a speaker, you also work with an allotted amount of time and a specific amount of material to present; you must usually hurry on even when an obstacle appears, if you are to get all the material presented. As a writer, you are not usually under such pressure. You can rewrite, revise, and polish the material, trying to get it as perfect as possible. Also, as a speaker, if you wish to refer to something you said much earlier, you must review it; as a writer, you need merely refer to the earlier page or chapter, and assume that the reader will also refer to that earlier section.

None of this changes the fact that for most people the word *presentation* is going to mean standing before an audience and speaking, but you should note the existence of writing as a means for making an effective presentation to a much larger audience than you could hope to reach from a platform. To review, here are just a few of the many kinds of written presentations you may be called upon to make or find useful for various purposes:

letters	brochures	newsletters
circulars	proposals	order forms
manuals	resumes	advertisements
catalog sheets	reports	releases

Let's go on now to Chapter 3 to discuss the purpose of all presentations, verbal or written: persuasion.

3

Persuasion, the Common Factor

Every presentation is designed to persuade, to sell something, even if only an idea or an image.

THE MANY FACES OF MARKETING

Marketing has achieved a faintly malodorous image of insincere, high-pressure selling. It is an undeserved reputation. Marketing, and its practical implementation as selling, is at the root of traditional American business and industrial success. Marketing is misunderstood by many who have somehow come to view this process as an intense effort, using high pressure tactics, to persuade the public into buying goods and services whether they need the goods and services or not. Most of us use the term only as a synonym for selling in its most basic sense. But marketing, in its broader sense, includes many more people: The seller of goods and services is by no means the only one who markets.

Everyone markets. The politician seeking your vote is marketing. The charity soliciting your donation is marketing. The hospital urging volunteers to contribute their services is marketing; so are the military organizations seeking recruits, the associations conducting membership drives, the societies urging you to turn out for meetings and attend conventions, the community college enticing you to attend evening courses, the volunteers outside the post office thrusting circulars at you,—even your spouse who wants you to stack the dishes in the dishwasher or run an errand.

Seen in this light, almost every exchange of words among us is a marketing effort of some sort, an effort to "sell" an idea or notion—to persuade another to believe and agree, if not to take some specific action. All presentations, whether they are oral or written, formal or informal, brief or lengthy, to an individual or to large groups, or delivered on any other basis, are an effort to persuade. Even when your presentation is not a sales presentation per se, it must sell—be convincing and persuasive—to be effective and successful. An awards presentation extols the virtues and accomplishments of the awardee to let the audience know that the awardee is worthy and merits the honor. If you were asked to orient a group of new employees to your company, you could hardly help but explain the benefits in a positive manner, to show the advantages of working for the organization. Even a training session involves a marketing effort: To instruct anyone in any subject, you must convince listeners that the instructions you offer are sensible and correct ones. For that matter, any speaker on any subject must come across believably as an expert or at least well-informed about the subject. Listeners must believe that you know what you are talking about. Achieving that believability must itself be an objective, and succeeding in the effort is a marketing achievement. You must have an objective if your presentation is to be coherent, and the effort to achieve an objective is itself marketing.

An essential requirement for preparing and delivering a presentation of any kind is your full recognition that your presentation must be persuasive. And to be persuasive, it must have certain qualities, of which none is more important than credibility.

CREDIBILITY

Believability, or credibility, is a necessity in all selling. The first major step in selling is arousing the prospect's desire for a promised benefit. A necessary second element is convincing the prospect that you can and will deliver the benefit—that is, that "buying" what you offer will result in getting and enjoying the benefit. Buying in this sense means accepting, not necessarily exchanging money. If your presentation is announced as "New Business Opportunities," attendees know from your title alone what it is that you promise as the general benefit. It will probably be assumed by the audience that the major stress will be on the adjective "new," and they will—justifiably—expect you to offer at least a few ideas that they have not heard of before. They will also expect those ideas to be true business opportunities that appear to be practical and not wild-eyed, implausible schemes. In short, you must make a promise of some benefit, enunciating that promise quite clearly, and you must then validate that promise with some proofs or evidence. Failing to deliver what you promised will disappoint your audience; that would hardly constitute a successful presentation.

Credibility is not a random factor or a quality that simply "happens;" it must be made to happen. It is the product of certain specific elements that produce it—or fail to do so. Here are some of the key factors that influence it.

The Promise

Credibility begins with the promise itself. A great many presenters make promises that seem to be too good to be true, and the conventional wisdom of skeptics is that if it sounds "too good to be true," it probably is not true. So promises of nearly instant wealth, for example, those programs who promise to show customers how to get rich quickly in real estate by buying residential and business properties with no money down, are of that "too good to be true" category. Many experienced real estate people shake their heads disdainfully at such promises and programs. Still, because so many people want to believe that promise, they attend the promoter's free seminars and watch the TV presentations, hoping to find persuasive evidence that the promise is not too good to be true but is a legitimate opportunity to change their lives. Note that when the promise is sufficiently appealing, many people will want to believe it. They will help you persuade them if you furnish a good opportunity to do so. You must put great thought into what you promise, even if it is a promise to be inferred from the title or the opening remarks of your presentation.

In the example used here, having aroused fond hopes with a seductive promise, the presenter offers a well-rehearsed program replete with convincers of many kinds, including his or her own confident manner and claims of personal success, detailed "explanations" of just how and why the listener can easily make it all come true, and testimonials from a few individuals who claim it all happened for them. Those are the proofs or evidence, and they buttress an already existing wish to believe. They *are not* necessarily true.

Reactive Skepticism

The passionate wish to believe works against the almost instinctive skepticism we usually feel toward great, sweeping promises. The degree of skepticism is directly proportional to the magnitude of the promise: It is not especially difficult to believe that you might be able to buy a modest home for yourself with little or no down payment. It is much more difficult to believe that you might buy a multimillion dollar office building with no money down. Still, if your wish to believe is strong enough, you may lend a most willing ear to an argument expounding that idea and even help the presenter prove the case.

You thus have two opposing forces: One, the wish to believe in promised benefits, and two, the natural skepticism. The two are in direct relationship—the greater the promised benefit, the greater the skepticism. But the greater the promise, the more intense the wish to believe.

Expertise Influences

Dottie Walters, an acknowledged authority in the field of professional public speaking, believes a speaker should be a true expert in his or her field. In *Speak and Grow Rich*, a book on professional/avocational public speaking, she and her co-author, her daughter Lillet, urge the reader to pursue 12 steps to becoming an expert, from studies in libraries to subscriptions to magazines and other sources of information. When you speak at length, your expert knowledge or the lack of it reveals itself readily enough and results in the audience's reaction to you and what you state in your presentations.

Initially, your listeners will take it for granted that you are an expert in whatever topic you are to present. They assume that you would not be on the platform before them if you were not reasonably expert or in possession of the pertinent facts. But they will be entirely willing and ready to change that assessment if you give them reason to—if you appear in any way to be less than fully qualified to speak to them on the subject. If you state as facts assertions that you cannot substantiate or that the audience knows to be untrue, it will constitute an immediate assault on the credibility of your presentation, as well as on your own personal credibility as an authority. If you falter and appear to be uncertain, the result will be a weakening of the initial confidence the audience conferred on you. If you are vague and rambling, you will appear to be less than truly knowledgeable. If your presentation consists entirely of generalizations, with no specific facts, details, or "for instances," it will be weakened. You are usually given the gift of credibility by your audience at the outset, but that does not relieve you of the need to validate that gift and prove it well-deserved.

Accuracy

You must be sure of your facts. Guessing is likely to result in misstatements that will undermine your credibility swiftly. This is even more true for written presentations because they become permanent records, easily referred to subsequently. (When Franklin D. Roosevelt made certain ill-advised campaign promises in an address in Pittsburgh, Pennsylvania, his advisors lamented that he had made them. But referring to the fact that they were mere words falling on air—it was before TV and tape recorders—his advisors sardonically suggested that he escape his unfortunate words by denying that he had ever been in Pittsburgh!) President George Bush could not, however, escape his frequent "read my lips" assurances that he would not raise taxes. Be sure to check all your facts in advance. If you are compelled to improvise or answer questions and are not absolutely sure of your facts when doing so, state that to your listeners. You might promise to check the facts later or suggest a source for researching them, but be cautious about making positive statements when you are not really sure.

Specifics

To be credible, you must be specific and precise in what you state and what you advocate. Suppose your presentation is on how to run a business from one's own home. Among other things, you wish to explain how to take advantage of the tax laws to write off some portion of a residence as a business expense. It is quite easy to anticipate the questions that would result almost immediately if you attempted to cover all of this with the bare statement that you can write off space used for business and said no more on the subject. Listeners would want to know just how much space can be written off, how to decide what space and other costs one is entitled to write off, how to make associated allocations of costs, and a host of related questions. You must thus describe and explain exactly the concept of exclusivity of use, as applied to space dedicated for office or other business use. Show on a blackboard or via some other visual medium exactly how to determine what portions of various expenses may be allocated for business and deducted and how to calculate the amounts to write off. Show an example or two, and cover marginal cases. Invite questions about cases you have not been able to anticipate. Anticipate the obvious or typical situations and plan to provide the answers to those in your planned presentation. You may get further questions even then, but you will have made the obvious questions and answers unnecessary.

Details

Your credibility can often be in direct proportion to the specific details you provide. An audience finds the inclusion of painstaking detail to be highly persuasive because, as the opposite of generalization, it makes your presentation believable. It is somewhat similar to the problem of asking a stranger for directions when you are in a strange town. The advice of a stranger who says something such as, "Go about a half-mile down this road, then turn left, and you'll find it," is not very reassuring. More reassuring directions would be, "Go down this road roughly a half-mile to the fire station. Right beyond that turn left on the first road—it's a narrow blacktop and not marked, so be careful you don't miss it. Then watch for the Miller Dairies on your right. Fletcher's general store is right next to Millers."

Audiences listening to you speak or reading your writing are no different. The inclusion of detail plays a large part in establishing your credentials as a true expert. To be persuasive, your presentation must be several leagues above the level of Saturday afternoon discourses on football strategy.

Audience Interests

Focus your presentation entirely on the interests of the audience. I once shared the platform with a gentleman who was quite expert in our field and a good speaker in many respects: He made an excellent personal appearance, was completely at ease on the dais, possessed a fine speaking voice, and had excellent delivery. What he did not exhibit was a sense of why he was there. Instead of using his personal experiences as anecdotes to illustrate his points, he used them to trumpet his achievements and to drop important names. It was small wonder that the audience savaged him in the post-presentation evaluation report.

Don't lose sight of why the two of you, you and your audience, are here. They came to get information and/or entertainment, the benefits they were promised, and you came for the fee, prestige, public relations, approval, and/or personal satisfaction. You have pledged to deliver those promised benefits, and you must do so. Your presentation cannot possibly be persuasive if it disappoints your listeners by failing to address their interests and failing to deliver what was promised them.

Empathy

Empathy can help you to understand your listeners' needs and to provide the necessary details of any point you make. It compels you to demonstrate your understanding of their views and your concern for them and for what they have to say. You listen attentively to their questions and wait patiently until they are finished before answering. When you display those qualities, you quickly forge a bond with your audience.

Your Platform Personality

So far we have discussed logical elements in the matter of delivering a credible presentation. There is at least one other highly important element that has nothing to do with logic, but is entirely emotional and subjective. It is the impact of your persona on the audience, how they feel about you on the basis of watching and listening to you. (I have covered much of this indirectly in the previous discussions, but it is important to talk to this directly and understand it fully.)

We fallible humans make our judgments as much on subjective/emotional/psychological grounds as we do on rational/objective ones. We have trouble being critical of someone we like, and are equally reluctant to approve the efforts of anyone who has rubbed us the wrong way. The personality you reveal to listeners—or what listeners perceive as your personality—has much to do with your success on the platform.

That latter qualification is critical. We rarely see ourselves as others see us. You may think that you are the strong, assertive, self-confident type—a good image. But suppose an audience sees you as dogmatic, combative, weak, evasive, arrogant, contemptuous, or otherwise someone not to be admired or respected? That is not an image that generates trust or affection. It is helpful to have an audience like you, if at all possible, but it is much more important that you are not disliked or mistrusted by your audience. You must radiate leadership, and that stems primarily from the ability to inspire a reasonable degree of respect, even admiration. An audience should be regarded as you would regard customers or prospective customers, even if you are not making a sales presentation per se. Key to this is to understand that the only truth, as far as the audience is concerned, is *their truth*, what they perceive as fact. In practical terms, it ought to be your truth too, for it is the only truth you have to work with.

Empathy enters the picture here, too. It is difficult not to like someone who shows a genuine concern for and understanding of your own needs and interests. But that is certainly not all there is to the matter of a suitable platform personality; there is more to it, much more, and the subject will come up again and again. You need to understand at least these important aspects of a good platform personality:

- Enthusiasm is a positive characteristic and a contagious emotion. It reflects your enjoyment in and zest for your subject. It should come across that you are delighted to share the information with your audience and working hard to be sure that you get the information across. If you happen to be one of the laconic, laid-back types, rarely raising even an eyebrow, much less your voice, work at changing your style on the platform, and let the audience know that you truly enjoy what you are doing and are working hard to succeed in it. You may laugh at deadpan comedians who appear to be bored to death to be standing before you telling funny stories, but you laugh with—not at— comedians who are obviously having a wonderful time entertaining you—Bob Hope, George Burns, Red Skelton, and Johnny Carson, for example. They obviously like talking to you. They like you, and it is obvious that they do. They radiate warmth.

- Gestures and facial expressions help in several ways. They make the presentation a graphic one, helping to drive home specific points and make them far more memorable. It is well-known that we humans retain only a small fraction of what we hear. When it is accompanied by some visual aid or illustration, the retention improves a bit because the point is registered with the eye as well as the ear. But gestures and grimaces— scowling, smiling, grinning, rolling your eyes, feigning astonishment or unbelief, waving your arms, shouting, whispering, pointing, and other nonverbal communications also "humanize" your presentation while also spicing it up a bit in stressing important points. (Who wants to listen to an expressionless speech delivered in a monotone?) These graphic enhancements punctuate your presentation, and they add to the enjoyment an audience gets from watching you, as well as listening to you. As Ed McMahon most correctly perceived, "It's all show biz."

- Look at individuals. Meet their eyes. But don't focus on any one or two in the audience; look all of them in the eye. Move your eyes about the entire room. Make it clear that you are talking *to* them, not *at* them. If you are a bit nervous on the platform, this will help you see how friendly most of the faces out there really are: Smile at them, and they will smile back.

- Use humor with great caution, if at all. Be careful about ethnic jokes or jests concerning handicaps, politics, sex, or religion; all are dangerous subjects to joke about. If anyone is to be the butt of your humor, make it yourself. It's easy to like someone who can laugh at his or her own misadventures and foibles. But don't use humor for the sake of humor. Use it only when it is directly appropriate to your point. (I never—well, practically never—use typical comedians' jokes or stories, but I do willingly relate some of my own maladroit, foolish, and often embarrassing mistakes when they illustrate a point. For an excellent resource on using humor in presentations, read Michael Iapoce's *A Funny Thing Happened on the Way to the Boardroom*.)

- Don't go to the extreme of being a clown. You must still command respect when on the platform, and buffoons may amuse, but they do not inspire respect or admiration. You must be sensitive to that careful balance between good-natured humor and undignified antics that make you appear foolish.

- Move freely about the platform. Don't hide behind the lectern. Many speakers invade the audience space. (I do, especially when I am trying to hear a question from some soft-spoken person in the back of the room.) Make it obvious that you are very much at ease and feel yourself to be among friends. Help your listeners to relax by making it clear that you are relaxed.

- Don't be afraid to be vulnerable or to show that vulnerability. It is part of being human, and it helps to establish a bond with the audience. One method I use to demonstrate this willingness to admit vulnerability is that of amusing listeners with tales of my own misadventures, as mentioned earlier. Another is welcoming challenges. When I invite questions, as I do at the outset of my seminars, I also invite challenges. I make it clear that I ask no one to accept what I say merely because I have said it. I welcome challenges from any who disagree with me, and I am entirely willing to discuss any matter that is at issue.

- Having respect for your audience and showing it is also essential. When a challenge does arise, as it does occasionally, I accept it as a sincere disagreement. I listen attentively to the other person and respond with an open mind. It is important to do so. It reflects respect for the individuals in your audience, and you cannot expect to earn their respect without returning it. The same show of respect should greet anyone with a question. Be careful that you never appear to be brushing aside any question, comment, or challenge, even trivial ones, from anyone in your audience.

4

At Ease on the Dais

The bad news is that it is quite likely that your knees will turn to water, your voice will rise to a shrill squeak, and your pores will leak profusely, even at the prospect of climbing to the platform. The good news is that nervousness on the speaking platform is not a rare disease, and there are cures that will work for you too.

ARE YOU A LALIAPHOBIC?

The fear of speaking—*laliaphobia*—is often credited with being the number-one fear of a majority of people. David Wallechinsky's *The Book of Lists* reported that 41 percent of a group polled on their greatest fears placed the fear of public speaking before their fears of heights, insects, financial woes, deep water, sickness, death, flying, loneliness, and dogs. Where do you fit in this hierarchy of common fears? You are not unusual if you dread the walk up to the dais; you are in excellent company, along with many well-known professional speakers, entertainers, and other public figures in many fields.

Some refer to this fear of facing an audience as nervousness or *speech anxiety*. A more common and perhaps more accurate term for this fear is *stage fright*. That suggests that the fear is not of speaking per se, but of appearing before an audience in a formal or semiformal situation—that is, on a platform or before an assembled group, even a small group, as the center of attention, with dozens of eyes fixed on you.

Common as this fear is, most individuals who are fearful of more formal speaking situations are totally at ease telling some story or "sounding off" confidently on some subject to a group in a cocktail lounge, living room, or other informal social gathering. Here, you are thoroughly relaxed and thoroughly at ease being the center of attention for a few minutes.

Why is the impact different? Is it because the informal setting puts you at ease? Because here you speak spontaneously and have not had time to get nervous with anticipation? Because you are with close friends? Because you are only for a few minutes the center of attention?

Whatever the reason—and all of the above speculations are relevant—let's analyze it a bit more in depth. To handle this fear, it is helpful to have a better understanding of it. It probably helps also to know that professional speakers and performers share this fear. In fact, many, perhaps even most, claim they are never without "butterflies" or "weak knees" when they perform. Some—Steve Allen, for one—even point out that the anxiety is not truly stage fright because it begins long before one must mount a stage and stand before an audience; it begins the moment you agree to do so and begin to contemplate the ordeal, possibly even regretting accepting the invitation. As consultant/seminar leader David Peoples observes, " . . . when the time approaches, you find yourself wishing for laryngitis, a snowstorm, a closed airport, or some other divine providence to spare you the ordeal." Many well-known performers, such as Helen Hayes, Luciano Pavarotti, Sir Lawrence Olivier, and even the jovial weatherman who appears to be so relaxed, Willard Scott, freely confess that they have never gotten completely over their stage fright, and they approach every performance with butterflies nervously dancing in their stomachs. I also have never overcome that nervousness completely. I have no conscious or rational fear of the platform, and I accept speaking engagements unhesitatingly. Yet I freely confess to experiencing butterflies in my stomach. The feeling vanishes quickly when I see the welcoming smiles of my audience and feel the warmth of friendly greeting.

ROOT CAUSES OF FEAR

Perhaps you have already experienced the fear of speaking generally. You found the prospect of speaking before a group in a formal or semiformal situation something that makes your throat dry and your palms sweaty. Those are subjective reactions, emotional ones. But there are more precise definitions of your anxiety, and getting a more precise and rational understanding is one step toward helping you overcome your fears. Try to precisely define what you really fear. The following list might help you:

1. You fear that you do not have a good "speaking voice" and thus you will come across poorly, as an amateur and failure, forever marked so.

2. You fear that you will fumble, go blank and forget what you are supposed to say, and become a laughing-stock. You are sure that you will be embarrassed and never able to show your face again.

3. You are sure that you will jeopardize your social or business standing by making a fool of yourself. Who will respect you after you have shown yourself to be the dolt who had the audacity to present him- or herself as a speaker?

4. You can't believe that you have anything to say that others will think worth hearing; your audience will go to sleep before you and applaud only because you have finished boring them to death.

5. You are sure that you will make some kind of foolish error and offend or alienate many people.

6. You think that you have been "getting by" pretty well so far, but you fear that on a public platform you will be exposed as a fake.

These are all commonly experienced anxieties. Many speakers do not have a particularly melodious voice. In fact, some highly successful speakers and performers have voices that are shrill, raspy, lisping, and otherwise far from capable of issuing the melodic "pear-shaped tones" posed as ideal. That is really irrelevant. As to fumbling or going blank, yes it happens, even to the most practiced and most professional performers making live appearances. But they go on, improvising and sometimes even capitalizing on it, but always carefully avoiding making an issue of it. Quite often, when something of this sort happens, the audience never even knows it! With practice, you will learn to handle such mishaps without pausing. Most of our worst fears never occur.

If you dread committing some awful blunder that may cause your listeners to laugh at you—not with you—you are certainly not alone. That is among the most common reasons for stage fright. It is like meeting her (or his) parents for the first time: You are all but certain that they will not like you or think you at all suitable as a mate for their offspring. You think that you may very well somehow "say the wrong thing," dress improperly for the occasion, or simply appear to be stupid. It never occurs to you that perhaps those parents will be delighted that their offspring was fortunate enough to win such a charming and delightful mate as you.

Avoid negative thinking, even though this is the first impulse most of us have. We live with terrible doubts, and many of us have a strange desire to underrate ourselves, to think of ourselves as impostors or fakes, a phenomenon lately recognized by specialists in the field of psychology as the *impostor syndrome*.

The Impostor Syndrome

One of the phenomena of the human psyche is the notion entertained by many successful people, especially the outstandingly successful ones, that they are impostors. They get the notion that they have been mistakenly credited with greater talents and achievements than they deserve, or have been the beneficiaries of mistaken identity. They fear that they will one day, perhaps at any minute, be exposed, revealed as fakes, undeserving of their reputations and honors. Ironically, this is more a fear that the most celebrated individuals have to an even greater extent than those of us with more modest achievements. It seems to exist in some proportion to the degree of success or celebrated status of the individual. But most who have achieved a respectable degree of success are susceptible to this syndrome. They are short-changing themselves in most cases, with inadequate self-images. Probably the fear is rooted in some basic insecurity the individual has and is usually totally unjustified. (Rare indeed are those who have no insecurities in this stressful and competitive society.) This is a common enough phenomenon, and you must ask yourself if you are one of those who suffers from this syndrome, even to a limited degree, thereby doing a gross injustice to yourself.

The problem of platform paralysis is well known, and a problem that, once identified, can be kept under control. We'll now consider how to overcome the problem and become a first-rate, polished presenter, making professional presentations.

A Few General Cures for the Problem

There is no single cure for the problem of laliaphobia, stage fright, nervousness, speech anxiety, butterflies, or whatever one chooses to call that attack of weakness before speaking in public. What works for me or for someone else may not be at all effective for you. You have to find your own cure, but trying what works for someone else may help you. One way to break into public speaking is by degrees, rather than by being thrown abruptly into the stream. That is, there are many kinds of pubic speaking situations, some less stressful than others. If it is possible to start your public speaking career under the least stressful conditions, by all means do so. Eventually, even if you never get completely over your nervousness (many leading speakers and performers never do), you will find it much reduced and much more endurable.

Misery Loves Company

It is much less stressful to be part of a panel of speakers, appearing together on a platform, especially seated (as is the typical case of guests on the shows of Phil Donahue, Geraldo Rivera, Sally Jesse Raphael, Oprah, and others). If you can arrange to get your feet wet in public speaking in this manner, you will learn to control and surmount your stage fright by easy stages. Note that I did not say the stress or nervousness will disappear entirely; it may do so, but not for everyone. However, it should diminish considerably with just a bit of practice at being in the limelight even on a limited scale.

Shields and Barriers

Interposing a shield or barrier between you and the audience is a great help for many nervous speakers. You may cringe behind the lectern for a few minutes to collect your thoughts, but you cannot make an effective presentation that way. Hide there for a few minutes, if you must, while you compose yourself and gain control, but then you must emerge and take center stage, weak knees or not. However, if the situation lends itself to speaking while you are seated behind a table, do so; that is almost as comfortable and reassuring as being part of a panel seated behind a table.

Using Distracters

The use of presentation aids of various kinds—verbal (audio tapes, video tapes, and demonstrations) and nonverbal (posters, models, chalkboard, transparencies, slides)—is designed to aid you in making your most important points and to aid the audience in understanding what you are presenting to them. But they also relieve stress for you. A large part of the stress is due to your acute sense of being the center of attention. The spotlight is on you, and dozens of pairs of eyes and ears are watching and listening to you. Distracting their attention by diverting it to something else, while also resting your voice, in some cases, is a relief. It is an especially welcomed relief when you are overly tense and nervous. You need to break that tension, and these are wonderful devices for doing so. Take advantage of them by using as many as you can manage to work into your program.

Preparation

One cause of acute stress is a feeling of being unprepared. I confess that I (and probably many others about to mount the dais) usually have the uneasy feeling that I am not fully prepared, even when I am going to present a seminar that I have presented hundreds of times before. However, if I were truly unprepared, I would be a great deal more than merely nervous; I would be in sheer terror, in panic. The knowledge that you are properly prepared is probably the most essential requirement and the greatest comfort.

Preparation means that you have done several things:

- You have planned your presentation carefully, whether it is a 20-minute speech or an all-day seminar. You prepared a completely detailed outline, as the minimum amount of material on paper, along with all presentation aids you are going to use, if any.

- You have created and prepared whatever mnemonic (memory assisting) devices you need, such as cue cards.

- You have your presentation aids organized for use in their proper sequence.

- You have rehearsed carefully. That does not mean that you have memorized your material, for you should not do that unless you happen to be a gifted actor who can make memorized material sound as though it were

spontaneous. Most of us sound like robots when we recite memorized material. Rehearsal for us means going
over the material again and again until we are sure that
we have mastered it so well that we can, in fact, speak
spontaneously and present everything in that manner.
You should have an especially precise plan for your
opening and closing, the two most critical elements of
your presentation. It is comforting and reassuring to
know that you have an opening that gets attention and
alerts your audience to just what to expect. It is equally
comforting to know that you have a dynamite finish
that leaves them impressed and forces them to applaud
you. (That is worth all the agonized fear and trembling.
As the late Jackie Gleason was so fond of saying with
such glee on many occasions, "How sweet it is!")

- You have attended to all the logistics to ensure that
everything is as you want it to be. For example, you have
seen to it that anything you did not personally carry to
the site of the presentation—handouts, presentation
aids, or other such material—was delivered there and is
waiting for you. You also saw to it that the room is set up
theater style or classroom style, whichever is most
appropriate for you; that there is a chalkboard, overhead projector, slide projector, screen, and/or any other
equipment you need; and that the lights, air conditioning, and public address system work. You have also seen
to it that there are pitchers of ice water available, and
refreshments if the program includes those. You have
drawn up a list of your requirements and gotten the list
to whomever is to take care of the physical arrangements. But you did not stop there. You got to the location well ahead of the audience and personally checked
it all out to verify that everything was in order. You also
wrote your own introduction and saw to it that you met
with and made arrangements with whomever was to
introduce you. When you mount that dais, you know
that all is in order. Unexpected calamities may occur—
the public address system stops working, the lights do

not perform as expected, the air conditioning breaks down, there is a chorus of coughers in the audience, there is loud noise from a too-loud meeting in the adjoining room, and a dozen other mishaps interfere with the smooth progression of your program, but you have at least checked everything out in advance and minimized the probabilities.

Confidence

A great many jokes have been made about that elusive quality called "positive thinking," but the jokes are usually told by those who lack it. If you are a true positive thinker you are rarely, if ever, "down." You wake up smiling, eager for a new day. You are an optimist. You believe that all will be well. You believe in yourself. You like most people, and you can't imagine that anybody does not like you.

You may call that quality confidence or self-confidence; it is also a sense of security. Perhaps we all have some degree of insecurity, but the greater your feeling of security, the less likely you are to be nervous on the dais.

How do you acquire or develop this trait? It *is* possible to develop an attitude that helps breed confidence in yourself. One way that is especially appropriate for you as a speaker is to prepare so thoroughly that nothing that happens can stump you or even slow you down: You know your subject cold: You can handle, without hesitation, any question or challenge coming from your audience. You have attended to all the large and small details of the meeting and presentation and prepared to cope with any unexpected problems. You have done your relaxation exercises before mounting the platform. You are ready to face your audience.

HOW THE PROFESSIONALS DO IT

Dottie Walters, who is not only herself a widely experienced speaker in demand all over the world, but has also worked with thousands of other professional speakers, has her own methods for coping with nervousness. She happens to be a happy person who truly likes people—one of those thoroughly upbeat personalities—and she stands on the dais and basks in the warmth of all those *friends* seated out there. She thinks warm and comfortable thoughts as she surveys the room. And, as do most professionals in the speaking business, she stresses the need for careful and complete preparation.

Popular presenter Ron Hoff recommends a 5-minute brisk walk before beginning as a help to steady trembling knees. He urges the nervous speaker to deliberately let muscles go limp as a relaxation exercise. That happens to be a first step in auto-suggestion (self-hypnosis) too, and makes a great deal of sense.

Some professionals believe that nervousness is a positive characteristic, a helpful condition. Consultant David Peoples, a popular seminar leader, says that it starts the adrenalin pumping and that it gets your "butterflies flying in formation."

Claudyne Wilder, president of a Boston management consulting firm, recommends eating sparsely on the day you are to make a presentation. She also recommends that you psyche yourself up by reviewing in your mind all the good qualities of your presentation—excellent examples, thoroughly organized information, good illustrations and aids, and whatever else you can justifiably take great pride in offering.

My own view is that nothing is as effective in relieving nervousness as is a real passion for your subject and great enthusiasm in presenting it. The nervousness stems from concern about yourself—how *you* appear, how well *you* speak, how well *you* dress, when it should be on how well *they* understand what you are saying, what *their* problems are or may be in mastering the skills you teach, what you can do to make things easier for *them.* When you begin to think that way— when you focus your entire attention, energy, and effort directly on helping your listeners grasp what you are saying and/or master the subject—nervousness is totally forgotten. Become an evangelist for your subject, a fanatical believer in it. Then you will concentrate entirely on ensuring that you are delivering the information and helping your listeners master it. Let yourself get carried away with your passion and enthusiasm; you'll quite soon forget about yourself entirely. You'll lose all consciousness of self, and begin to use your arms, make gestures, raise your voice, and become quite animated without even realizing it. Don't try to plan or rehearse the gestures and inflections; if you feel strongly enough about the subject and the points you are trying to make, those things will come about naturally, without planning and without conscious effort. In fact, if someone were to make a videotape of you on the platform you would be stunned: You would not believe that it was really you stoking up the audience's enthusiasm to match your own. Nervousness? What's that? You can't be nervous when you have completely forgotten everything except watching the audience as you speak to spot any signs of doubt, confusion, failure to understand, disagreement, or other such reactions; you will soon become quite sensitive to these, and you will respond to them.

5

Presentation Aids
Relieve the Stress

Most presentations benefit greatly from the use of presentation aids. Many such aids are available and in common use. But there are a great many things to be considered in the selection and use of these aids, perhaps far more than you might have believed.

WHAT IS A PRESENTATION AID?

We tend to think automatically of a presentation as an exercise in public speaking. The term *presentation aid* thus tends to conjure up an image of something to supplement and explain words uttered from the platform. While the majority of presentations are public speaking performances, there is also a *written* presentation, which will be discussed in this chapter.

Presentation aids are used in both written and delivered presentations. The following list of presentation aids are commonly used. A few are relevant to only the classic presentation delivered from the platform, but most have relevance to and are used in written presentations also. The kinds of items you are most likely to find useful or necessary as presentation aids include:

flip charts	posters	props
models	slides	transparencies
videotapes	audiotapes	handouts
movies	chalkboards	filmstrips
tables	diagrams	matrices
miscellaneous devices	leave behinds	demonstrations

A few of the items listed may need a word of explanation. They will be discussed at greater length as specific examples are cited. "Props," for example, refers to any devices other than those used directly to illustrate or explain a point, but yet useful for stressing a point. You might ring a loud bell if you are discussing fire alarms or strike a block with a judge's gavel to dramatize a point in a presentation where the gavel or symbol of the judicial bench is relevant or analogous. (Raymond Burr, doing an insurance commercial on TV, used a pair of handcuffs to illustrate the point of avoiding being "locked in.") The use of such devices dramatizes the points or meaningful analogies and makes them especially memorable.

"Miscellaneous devices" refers to a wide assortment of special aids, many of them patented and proprietary, such as one that has cards that can be moved about a background board to illustrate various options and alternatives of organization or process.

"Leave behinds" are materials you give out to the audience at the end of the session and leave with them, such as a brochure or a manual that documents the presentation. Leave behinds are also handouts, but handouts may be aids that are an integral part of the presentation.

Demonstrations are another way of dramatizing or illustrating some important elements of your presentation and driving points home with special emphasis. You may conduct or make a demonstration (1) entirely on your own, (2) with the help of an assistant or two, (3) have an assistant perform the demonstration, or (4) draw on volunteers from the audience. This last way is often the most beneficial.

One of the aids listed is aural only, several are visual only, and the others are audiovisual. This suggests one way of classifying them, which we will discuss a bit later.

Presentation aids are used for two general purposes: The primary one is to help the listener (or reader) understand a concept or point that is not easy to grasp from a verbal explanation alone. This may be done by presenting an analogy or example—or, if you want to help the listener visualize something, a graphic illustration. The other common use of a presentation aid is to dramatize or otherwise stress a point to ensure that the listener's attention is directed especially toward it and make the concept or point more memorable. There are other benefits of using such aids, and you will hear more about these "spinoff" benefits as you read through this book.

REDUCING STRESS

In an earlier chapter, we discussed the benefits of using presentation aids as one means for reducing nervousness on the platform. That was, of course, a selfish view, considering only your needs as the presenter, and not the needs of your listeners. Their needs should take priority, and the true purpose of using presentation aids is or should be first to aid the listeners in grasping your messages and meanings with minimum difficulty, and second to aid yourself in making your presentation maximally effective.

The stress in the room is often dual: Listeners who came to gain important ideas and instructions often must strain to master everything presented. Their anxiety is different from yours, but it is real, nevertheless. Words wafted across the room are transient; the listener strains to hear them, to understand them, and to remember them—to learn. How well is he or she able to do this? Not well at all, according to most sources if only spoken words are used.

We learn between 75 and 90 percent of all we know through our eyes. Hence the need for visual aids in making presentations more effective. Our ears play at best a secondary role in learning. However, the most effective learning is the result of seeing and hearing simultaneously. We use this principle throughout this book.

CHOOSING WHICH PRESENTATION AID TO USE

The subject matter of your presentation should affect or even dictate the primary medium. For instance, how much could you learn about sculpture or painting from sound alone, without seeing many examples? On the other hand, how much could you learn about music appreciation without sound? Would not hearing many examples be absolutely essential here? Consider for yourself which—sound, sight, or both—are of predominant importance in presentations concerning theater arts, automotive design, writing, phonetics, and bird calls. (Or any other topics you wish to substitute for these.) You will soon see that the selection of media is not a casual matter subject to fixed rules. The nature of the subject is only the starting point for considerations underlying the conception, development, and use of presentations aids of various kinds. There are other important factors.

Audience Differences

The individual circumstances surrounding a given presentation also bear heavily on what should be used as a visual medium. One circumstance is the physical realities—size of group and available facilities. For example, a basic rule is that a visual medium is useful only if everyone in the audience can see it. If you address a group of many hundreds in a large auditorium, posters and flip charts will be of little use to those who are not seated in the first few rows and reasonably close to that portion of the stage where you have displayed the posters or flip charts. Even slides, filmstrips, and overhead transparencies may present a problem in that the screen must be large enough for the projections to be read in the far rows, but that may require a screen that is too large to be read comfortably by those close to it. Videotape, however, might work well here if there are enough monitors placed throughout the auditorium to enable everyone to see and hear the videotape.

The nature of the audience itself is another circumstance that may affect your choice and use of presentation aids. For example, you may find a few individuals with impaired hearing in any large group. But suppose they are a fairly elderly group, perhaps a group of retired people. It is then highly likely that there will be a good percentage of individuals with impaired hearing, and possibly impaired eyesight as well. You will have to choose your presentation aids and methods for using them quite carefully and thoughtfully in each case.

If you happen to be called upon to address an audience of foreign-born individuals, you may find that they speak and understand English far better than they can read it, a not unusual situation with such audiences. You must therefore restrict or possibly abandon selection and use of visuals that depend on text—even short phrases and, especially, idioms.

Presentation aids for offering data to a lay group is often best done via cartoons and other lighthearted graphics. Such an audience may very well be antipathetic to sober statistical presentations of any kind. However, if you address an audience of engineers, scientists, economists, or other professionals in a number of other highly organized and proceduralized specialties, you will find that they tend to want to see graphs, plots, and other kinds of charts based on specific data. They are accustomed to working with such aids and will grasp and accept information much more quickly and easily when these kinds of aids are used freely.

This latter kind of audience is likely to be also highly appreciative of tabular data:

Bean variety	Plants inoculated	Plants diseased
	Number	*Number*
Alaska	29	2
Alderman	25	11
Bonneville	19	6
Canner King	19	9
Delwiche Commando University of Wisconsin[1]	18	6
Glacier	21	14
Bountiful	8	7
Dwarf Horticultural	13	1
Great Northern University of Illinois[1]	3	5
Idaho Refugee	3	3
Michelite	5	12
Pinto	17	6

[1] Tests made in Illinois and Wisconsin.

You might assume that simple tables with messages explaining each block would be easy for anyone to grasp quickly, even if they had never been exposed to such representations. To the contrary, I have found, those unaccustomed to such pictorials or diagrams have difficulty understanding them, even when they are as straightforward as one showing the evolution of a maintenance manual depicted on top of page 61 (Figure 1).

A few of the many different kinds of pictorials that can be used to make up posters, slides, overheads (transparencies), or other visual aids to presentation are presented on the next few pages (Figures 2–7).

The names by which these various kinds of graphs and charts are known is not important. What is important is that you become aware of the many ways in which you can present

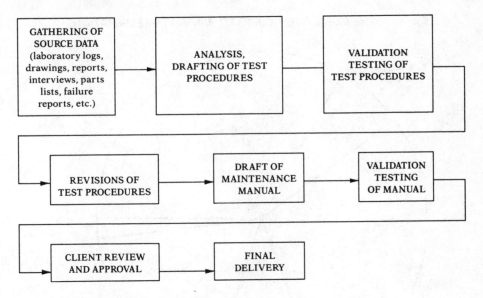

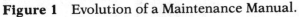

Figure 1 Evolution of a Maintenance Manual.

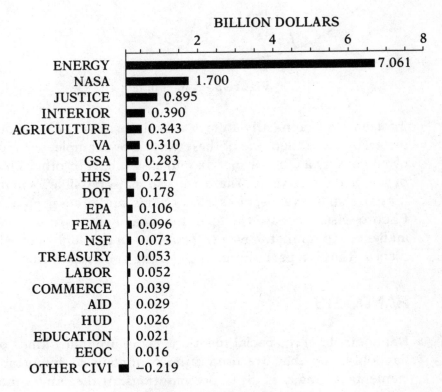

Figure 2 A bar chart.

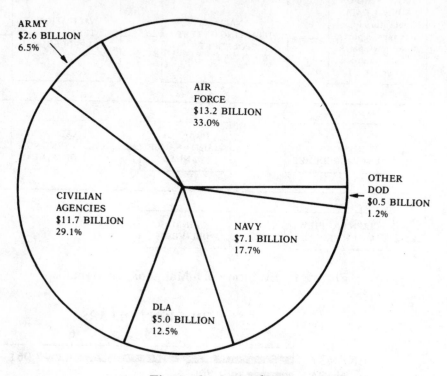

Figure 3 A pie chart.

information graphically. In fact, most information can be depicted by more than one of these ways. For example, you can often convert a table or matrix into a bar chart or other kind of graph and vice versa. There are also many possible formats for bar charts, graphs, plots, flow charts, and other graphics. Choose wisely; choose the form most easily grasped by *your* audience. To do that, however, you must understand your audience. That is a part of proper planning and preparation.

HANDOUTS

Handouts deserve special mention. There are many kinds of handouts, and they are used quite commonly as important elements for many kinds of presentations. At the same time, many of those who speak frequently endorse the use of handouts only reluctantly, and stress that handouts ought to be

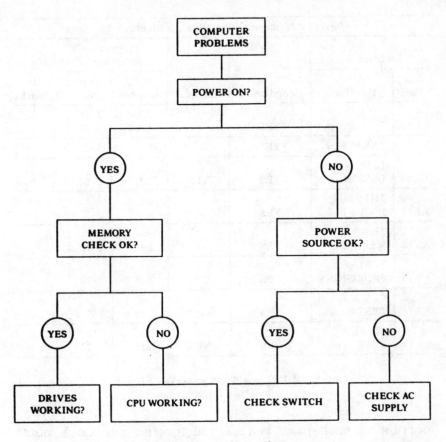

Figure 4 A flow chart.

used sparingly—only a few pages in size and passed out to attendees only when the session is over. The concern is that, with a handout before them, the audience will not give the speaker full attention, and will be distracted.

I have some trouble with the notion that I would be in competition with my own handouts and, what's worse, that I would lose to that competition! But perhaps some concern is there and that may be a force that drives me to be dynamite on the platform and not permit myself to be upstaged by my own creation!

I usually use a single handout; a small manual—in which I provide space for notes (see p. 175). Note that a generous

Matrix Table Showing Compliance with Elex-T-551

| Specification | | Compliance? | Exceeds? | Proposal Reference | | Title/ Remarks |
Par.	Title/Subj.			Par./ Graphic	Page No.	
3.5.8	Printer copy	YES	—	2.3, 1, 2.3, 2	2–14, 2–46	
3.5.9	TEMPEST	YES	—	3.1	3–1	
3.5.10	ELEC. DESIGN	YES	YES	2.3, 4	2–14	
3.5.11	THERMAL DESIGN	YES	—	2.5, 6, 8, 9	2–16, 2–17	
3.5.12	TEST MEASURE.	YES	—	2.13	2–18	
3.5.13	TEST PROVISIONS	YES	YES	2.15	2–20	
3.5.14	CLASS A TEST	YES	—	2.15	2–21	
3.5.17	CLASS B TEST	YES	YES	2.16	2–22	

Figure 5 A matrix.

portion of each page is reserved for the attendee's notes rather than providing empty pages at the end for notes. The less turning of pages, the less noise from your audience to compete with your voice. Having used such handouts for the past decade or so, I have had no reason to regret using them. In fact, they have been an aid to me in more than one way: The knowledge that each attendee will receive a manual documenting the presentation and serving as a permanent reference definitely encourages attendance. The manual is an important element to attendees. Most people giving up their time and spending dollars to attend a lengthy presentation do not like the idea of going away empty-handed or with a mere brochure or two. In those cases where an organization retains me to make a presentation to their members or staff, the inclusion of the handout has been inducement to their hiring me versus another consultant. I offer training presentations

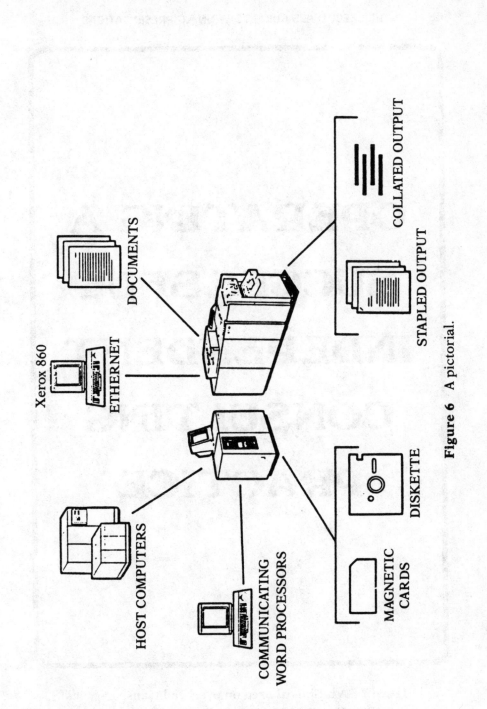

Figure 6 A pictorial.

Xerox 860

ETHERNET

DOCUMENTS

COLLATED OUTPUT

STAPLED OUTPUT

HOST COMPUTERS

COMMUNICATING
WORD PROCESSORS

MAGNETIC
CARDS

DISKETTE

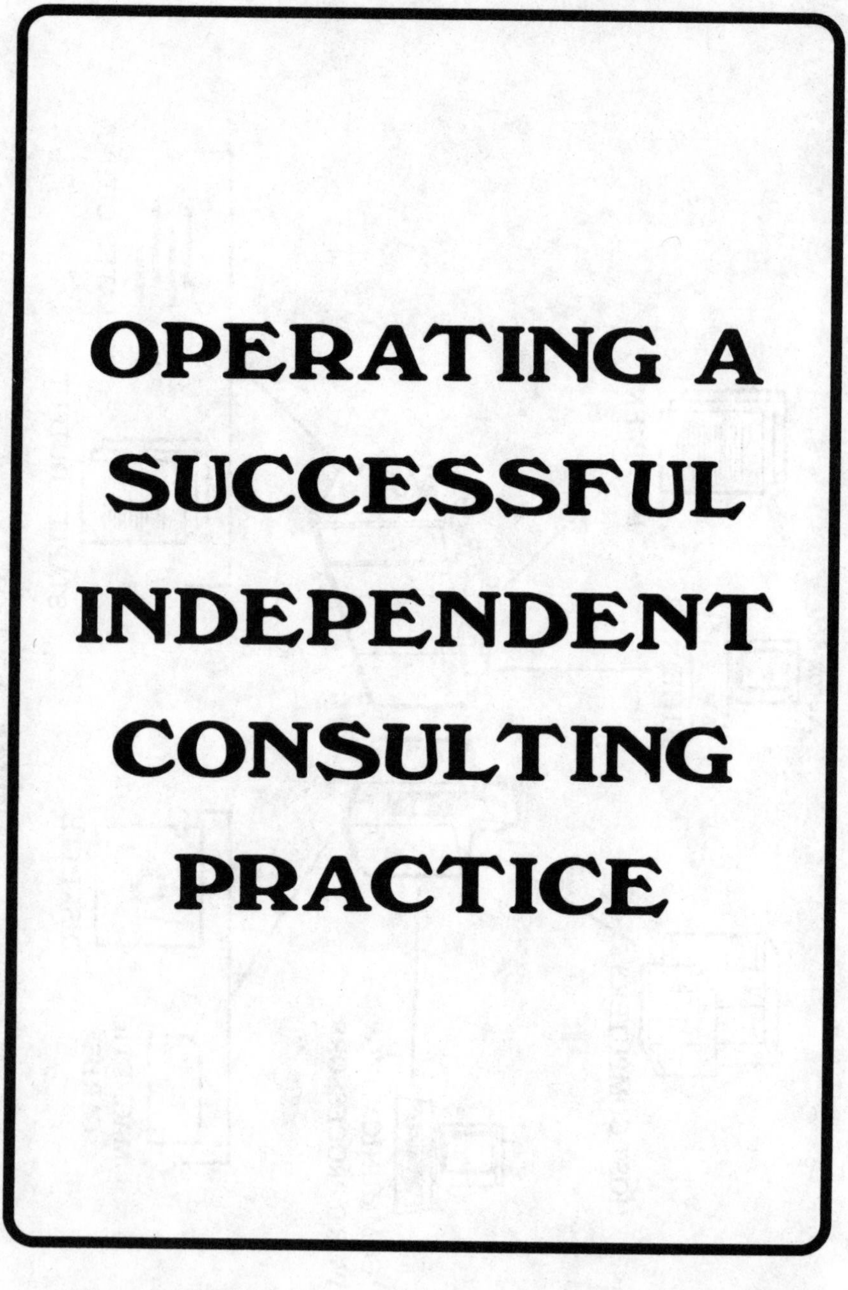

OPERATING A SUCCESSFUL INDEPENDENT CONSULTING PRACTICE

Figure 7 A billboard used on overhead transparencies to summarize or announce the topics to be discussed.

and the inclusion of a permanent reference issued to each attendee is quite a powerful inducement.

Handouts are especially useful in conjunction with all-day training seminars. I do not use handouts when I am simply delivering a speech (other than my business cards, when requested). That is an entirely different situation, and is probably the situation others have in mind when they recommend restricting the use of handouts.

Types of Handouts

Handouts can take a great many forms and formats. Here is a short list of ideas for handouts, which includes descriptions of many commonly used ones. Some are appropriate to any presentation, while others are relevant to only certain presentations and situations.

- *Manuals.* They can take the form of my own, as described, or any other form, bound with a corner staple, side stitched, in a plastic binder, in a looseleaf form, or any other form for any size you deem appropriate.
- *Commercially Published Books.* Many seminars include a commercially published book, often written by the leader of the seminar. (Many professional speakers who write and self-publish their books and tapes sell them at the seminar as a regular activity.)
- *Audiotapes and Videotapes.* These are less commonly used as handouts, but has been done.
- *Copies of the Transparencies.* Many speakers offer attendees a set of copies of their overhead transparencies, usually as black and white copies.
- *Outlines.* Some speakers provide attendees with a detailed outline of the presentation as an aid to following the continuity.
- *Exercise Sheets.* In seminars and workshops, especially the latter, exercise sheets of various kinds are

often handed out at appropriate times during the presentation.

- *Miscellaneous Assortments.* Some presentations, notably seminars, include as a handout a folder stuffed with miscellaneous items, such as public documents, brochures, booklets, pamphlets, and press releases. In fact, when I conduct seminars for organizations, under contract, the organization often adds materials of its own choosing to a folder that includes my manual.

When to Distribute Handouts

Experienced presenters who are opposed to handouts generally believe that if handouts *are* used they ought to be distributed at the close of the presentation. Many presenters do not want attendees taking notes and suggest that it may be preferable to advise attendees that note-taking is unnecessary because a handout will be distributed when the session ends.

I do not agree with that; I provide note-taking space in the handout manual, so that the attendee has his or her notes in a permanent reference. Nor do I believe that note-taking is ever unnecessary. Attendees may never look at their notes later, but the act of making notes helps greatly to impress the information in one's memory.

Some presenters use several handouts, distributing them at various times during their presentation, as they deem appropriate. This is probably most useful during seminar and workshop presentations. It has the disadvantage that it interrupts continuity and provides diversion of the attendees' attention.

Final Comments

The question of whether to use handouts and how to use them, if at all, has no single answer. You must judge for yourself whether it will be helpful to you and your audience, depending on the nature of your presentation, your objectives, and the circumstances. One unexpected bonus for me, I find, is that using the manual as a handout is a time-saver for me. Frequently, I can reduce the time needed to answer a question by pointing out that the question is answered in the manual. It may be useful to experiment with handouts and then judge what works best for you.

YOUR NEEDS FOR PRESENTATION AIDS

Writers often make the mistake of supplementing their words with graphic illustrations after the writing is completed. After they have finished writing their text, they then turn to consider where and how they may gracefully introduce a few helpful photographs, drawings, graphs, charts, or even matrices. That effort to supplement words with graphic illustrations is a classic cart-before-the-horse anomaly. The proper question, asked before one writes, is, "How or by what medium can this idea, concept, or image best be transmitted and explained?"

Don't Illustrate Your Words

This is as true for speakers as it is for writers. Graphic illustrations should never be used to supplement language. Quite the reverse: Words may be necessary to supplement graphics. You may have to use a bit of language to explain the drawing or the chart. Even then, the wise use of effective titles, captions, and legends will reduce that need. The item on page 61, however, was a functional flowchart of basic steps and procedures in developing a maintenance manual. A caption stating that would be all that is necessary to explain the chart.

The point is to decide first what point, idea, concept, or image you wish to convey, and then to judge whether words, written or oral, or some graphic illustration is better suited to convey it. "Better suited" refers to efficiency and effectiveness in delivering the message and in making it memorable.

The nature of the presentation aid you choose depends on several factors, as pointed out earlier, including the subject, the objective of the presentation, and the nature of the listener—what is likely to be most meaningful to and most readily grasped by the listeners. There is a final factor: What is possible or, at least, most practicable for you?

PRACTICAL CONSIDERATIONS

There are some practical considerations in the development and creation of presentation aids: You may be limited by whatever facilities are available to you. "Overheads," those 8-by 10-inch transparencies used with an overhead projector to cast an enlarged image on the screen, are extremely popular and have numerous practical advantages. Convenience is one: It is usually not difficult to arrange to have an overhead projector and screen available and the transparencies are small and quite light. Another convenience factor is that it is quite easy to rearrange the order in which you present the overheads or to go back to look at an earlier one again. Neither of these is as easy to do with some other kinds of aids.

There is also the ease of creating them: You can make a transparency in any ordinary office copier, using black lettering on the transparency. The transparency itself can be purchased in a variety of colors.

There was a time, when you would have had to hire a professional illustrator or have an outside service produce your overhead transparencies, if you wanted professional quality in them. Your alternatives would have been to settle for your own hand lettering and other artistic abilities or use a bulletin typewriter to get oversize lettering. Today, with the ready availability of desktop computers and related equipment and software, it is possible to produce your own transparencies, handouts, and even posters of excellent quality.

There is another way to use an overhead projector: You can use it as a chalkboard. You can write directly on the image surface with a marker pen, and wipe it clean with any good solvent.

Flip charts are also very popular. Some speakers use blank flip pages and write on them with a marker pen, using them as a chalkboard, but without the necessity for erasing the board: You simply flip to a clean page for the next one. Others have prepared charts, posters, and signs, in whatever order they wish to present them. Here again, you must either settle for your own artistic abilities or find someone who can do a better job than you can.

Slides have to be sent out to a photo lab to be made. In addition, you must darken the room to show them and be familiar with the slide projector. Despite the fact that you can get a great deal of information into a slide and show photographs as well as text and drawings, slides are not as popular as the other methods mentioned here.

Demonstrations are quite effective when it is practical to use them. In some situations, it is possible to have the entire audience participate in a demonstration. For example, in value engineering (also known as value analysis and value management), a series of seven questions must be addressed and answered. When the entire audience is involved on a voluntary basis in seeking answers to the basic questions—"What is it? What does it do?" and "What else would do that?"—a great deal of interest is generated. As a spinoff of this, challenging the audience works well, too. For example, in lecturing on marketing, I inform an audience that I doubt that any of them know what business they are in. It is a cold-water shock, of course. I wait a few minutes for the shock to register fully, while I offer the audience what I hope is a reassuring smile. I then set out to "prove" it (according to how *I* claim their businesses ought to be defined, of course). I invite volunteers to define their businesses for me. I then redefine those businesses according to the point I am trying to make. It is usually effective, as it gets every member of the audience involved and I get their full attention.

6

Typical Presentation Hazards: Expecting the Unexpected and Coping with It Successfully

Anything that can go wrong will.
—Murphy's Law

EXPECT THE UNEXPECTED

Murphy, of the famous Murphy's Laws, focused on the downside of everything. His many "laws," to which others have added so many modifications and additions, could best be summarized as predictions of the unexpected and unwanted as inevitable events. He assured us that anything that can go wrong will, even if going wrong seems to be the least likely event, and his other laws detailed and elaborated on that theme.

That sort of paradox—the probability that the improbable will happen—was the nightmare of early TV performers, when all performances were "live." Missed cues, props that didn't work, sets that collapsed, sound effects that fizzled, actors and actresses who forgot their lines, and scores of other minor and major disasters were responsible for selling a great many antacid remedies to nervous casts and production officials. The arrival of videotape reduced the live broadcasts to a handful; hardly any regularly scheduled shows other than news events are broadcast live today, so the many disasters never reach audiences (except later, in some cases, as "bloopers").

Leave Nothing to Chance, But . . .

In public speaking, you are in the same position as those early TV performers. You have prepared, rehearsed, and checked everything out personally. The public address systems and your lapel mike work perfectly. The air conditioning is set at the right level for the size of the room and audience you expect. You know where every control needed for lights and equipment are in the room, and you have checked to be sure that all the equipment is working. You have verified that your materials were sent out on schedule and have arrived in time for your presentation. You have written and sent on, weeks in advance, your own introduction for the individual who is to present you to the audience. You are quite expert in the topic you are to discuss, and exceedingly enthusiastic about it. Your voice and your smile are working well, and you are cool and confident. You are as ready as you will ever be to hold an audience, any audience, in the hollow of your hand. What could possibly go wrong?

Unfortunately, everything could go wrong. Murphy's laws are working overtime, once again proving his accuracy as a forecaster. Disaster awaits. For example,

- That introduction that you wrote so carefully for yourself and sent out weeks in advance either never arrived or was mislaid.

- Your introducer knows next to nothing about you, and is himself obviously not at all practiced nor comfortable on the platform. He stumbles and fumbles through a minute or two of evasive "uhs" and "ahs," mispronounces your last name, bestows on you a new and different first name, and finally flees the platform and leaves you with the shambles he has created.

- You now step forward to face a thoroughly confused and somewhat apprehensive audience. You can see it in their faces. They expect a plodding speech to follow that completely inept introduction, and they are almost hostile now or prepared to become so if you confirm their worst fears.

Unusual? Unfortunately, not at all. It happens all too often. Is it a disaster? Yes, but only if you permit it to be one. You can salvage the situation if you act promptly and skillfully to gain audience control.

Coping

The first requirement in this or any other emergency is to keep cool. Fight off panic, if you feel it, and don't let your dismay or frustration show. You may even turn this misadventure into an asset. Smile and thank your introducer as though he had been as silver-tongued an orator as William Jennings Bryan. Then proceed calmly. You have several choices: (1) You can proceed as originally planned and simply dispense with the introduction you should properly have had; (2) you can do your own introduction; or (3) you can make some light or jocular remark, such as, "Well, there is something to be said for brevity, isn't there?" with a knowing look or a roll of your eyes ceilingward that will arouse at least a chuckle from your audience. Be careful, however, that your remark does not sound bitter or angry. You should be striving to reflect good-natured amusement or even-tempered tolerance, if you choose not to totally ignore the incident. That will enlist the sympathy of your audience and establish a bond immediately.

But perhaps the information about you and your presentation that was to have been offered in introducing you is too important or necessary to your presentation to omit. In this case, you can supply the missing information directly or indirectly to your audience, as though you had so planned it. Of course, you cannot extol yourself and your many virtues as an introducer could have done, but you can work the information into your opening remarks. For example, I have said in such cases, "I hope you will forgive my immodesty, but you are entitled to know what my qualifications are for presuming to instruct you in winning government contracts." I then relate, as factually as possible, a few relevant achievements to make my point.

A good idea is to have a copy of your introduction always with you, ready to hand over to your introducer at the last minute if need be. As an alternative, it is a good idea to have some prepared remarks to handle the kind of problem we have been discussing here.

In general, even when the introduction is satisfactory, a light remark following it is not amiss. General Alexander Haig is not exactly a humorist, but he drew a good laugh from the audience at the Concord resort hotel in the Catskills during the few introductory skirmishes of his brief campaign for the presidency when he thanked his introducer as follows:

> Well, thank you, sir. That is easily the second-best introduction I have ever had. The best was when I was to speak in London and found my host had suddenly become ill, forcing me to introduce myself.

All Equipment Is Treacherous

I am fortunate in being rarely troubled by failures of public address systems and microphones. The reason is that I rarely make use of them. Unless my audience runs to at least several hundred people in size, I have no difficulty making my voice heard in the farthest reaches of the room. I have trained my voice to be resonant enough and powerful enough to serve most of my needs in public speaking. (I can also recommend a few years of wartime experience as a drill sergeant as excellent conditioning for the job!)

Anything you can do to make you independent of equipment is good insurance against Murphy's laws in the area of equipment malfunctions and failures. That is another reason for overheads being preferable to slides: They and the projector are relatively simple and thus less likely to give you problems. Flip charts, posters, and chalkboards are simpler yet and thus much greater proof against the curse of Murphy. I use overheads as a rule, but can always turn to the chalkboard and flip charts (blank ones, that is) if necessary to frustrate Murphy's efforts to frustrate me.

Plans A and B

A large part of the cure for any ills such as those just described is preparation: Be prepared to cope by anticipating trouble possibilities and having a Plan B to supplement and back up Plan A. I employ a simple philosophy in this regard: I try to determine, first of all, the elements over which I do not have direct or complete control. I then prepare back up plans against the possibility of failures and mishaps. My primary plan, Plan A, anticipates that all will go perfectly well. But Plan B, which is my "Murphy Plan," anticipates that nothing will go well, especially that which depends on anything not under my direct control. My Plan B has rescued me on many occasions; I never leave home without it.

Missing Materials

I dislike the necessity for shipping materials ahead, but I know that it is unavoidable in many cases. I can't drag heavy cases of books and other handouts about with me; there is no reasonable alternative to shipping them ahead to the hotel, meeting hall, or sponsor. However, I do what I can to minimize the difficulty. For one thing, I employ a small manual that I have written and copyrighted for my seminars. When I am retained by an organization to present a seminar to a group, I furnish the organization a single, master copy of the manual, with permission to reproduce by any means they wish enough copies for the seminar. They may add any other handouts they wish to, and often they do. That plan has worked well for me for years.

If your circumstances are such that you must ship materials ahead, check closely to see to it that the right materials have been sent. When you reach the place where you are to speak, check immediately on the materials to ensure that they have arrived and that they are the right materials. Finding that they have not arrived or that the wrong materials have been shipped is bad enough; learning this at the last minute is even worse. The earlier you know of a problem the better the chances that you will find a way to cope with it. On one occasion, a frantic call got the missing materials to the meeting room after the session started, disappointing but certainly not as bad as not arriving at all. If you are a speaker who wishes to do sales of books, tapes, or other material, the late arrival of the material won't really hurt you (the sales take place after the meeting), but non-arrival will be costly. Still, there is a remedy for that, too: Carry samples of whatever you wish to sell and a supply of order forms, so that you can take orders at the meeting for subsequent fulfillment. At least one speaker I know always sells his sets of audiotapes and texts in this manner, so he never has to ship the materials ahead.

Delayed and Missed Flights

Airline schedules can be unpredictable and unreliable. If you are to minimize the problems of missed flights and disastrous delays, you need to plan traveling ahead, with as much margin for error as possible. Try to arrive as early as possible so that there is time to change flights, if necessary, or perhaps call ahead and make arrangements to adjust the schedule when that is possible. If you miss a flight or the flight is delayed excessively, you may be able to get there by a less direct route with much less loss of time. When I was stuck in an Arkansas airport by a flight that had to be grounded for many hours for radar repairs, I was able to get to Albuquerque in time for my meeting by taking a flight to Dallas and changing planes there. Taking flights that are nominally out of the way—flying indirect routes to where you want to go—is the answer to many of these problems.

Sometimes chartering a flight is a good answer. When I missed my 4:00 P.M. flight to Atlanta at Dothan, Alabama, I found no other commercial flight out before midnight. However, it was possible to charter a small private plane (a Piper Cherokee) for only $40, and make it to Atlanta in time to connect with my regular commercial flight there.

I personally find flying an increasingly intolerable hassle, so whenever possible—going to locations only two to four hours away by road—I drive. It is part of my basic philosophy of maintaining as much direct control as possible. Probably this is not for everybody, for some individuals truly dislike driving, but it is much less stressful when you are in direct control.

Consider the possibility of using the train, too. Traveling between Washington, DC, and New York City, for example, is slightly less than three hours by the AMTRAK Metroliner. The flight is about 45 minutes, but the total elapsed time, city to city, is at least three hours also (and probably a bit longer), since travel to and from airports is a major time factor. Seating is much more spacious and comfortable on the train, and you can read or work in relative tranquility for a few hours.

HECKLERS AND OTHER PESTS

Hecklers are more likely to be found in audiences addressed by comedians than those gathered to hear a speaker, but they are certainly not unknown to speakers either. You are more likely to be heckled at evening presentations—during something such as a banquet or afterdinner speech—than during a seminar because hecklers are quite often individuals who have had a generous number of cocktails before your presentation.

Hecklers are generally of one of two varieties. One is the plain vanilla joker who is just having fun. He doesn't set out to destroy your presentation (I am saying "he," but it could be she), and there is no malice in his interruptions and loud remarks, but he does the damage nevertheless.

The other type is truly hostile, possibly because he is drunk and happens to be that type of drunk who gets nasty and belligerent, or possibly just antagonistic for some reason you cannot even surmise.

This is a difficult problem to deal with. Comedians can put down hecklers with caustic retorts, even getting an additional laugh or two from it. Experienced professional comedians often have a memorized stock of putdowns to silence a heckler. But it is dangerous for you to do so. The heckler may happen to be an important official of the organization who has simply had a bit too much to drink and intends only to show himself off as a humorist. Or a sharp putdown may escalate the heckling rapidly into a nasty confrontation. But even if the heckler is a complete stranger to everyone, evidently not truly hostile, and is obviously drunk, harsh comebacks will not reflect favorably on you. You must handle the situation with much more grace than that.

Just ignore the first remark or two from the heckler. He or she may be satisfied with that and subside for the rest of your presentation. It is well worth trying that tack first. Only if the heckler persists must you undertake some remedial action.

Dottie Walters recommends, among other measures, a light-hearted, good-natured semi-putdown, such as, "Excuse me, sir; I work alone," said with a grin. Alternatively, invade the audience space and continue speaking, while resting a reassuring hand on the heckler's shoulder as a direct suggestion to be silent. (That has the great advantage that it is not an interruption of your presentation.) As a variant of that, you might approach the heckler, take his hand, and thank him— with obvious good natured satire—for his contribution. That may satisfy him that he has gotten the attention he wanted or it may embarrass him slightly, encouraging him to be silent henceforth.

"Heckler" is an inexact term. Not all the several varieties of presentation pests intend to heckle you per se, although it may turn out to be heckling. But there are various types of meeting hall nuisances and troublemakers, each with his or her own agenda.

One such type of nuisance is the know-it-all expert. He has more education, more experience, more knowledge, and more wisdom than anyone in the room, he will assure you, directly or indirectly. He is on an ego trip. He really doesn't care much about the subject at hand or discussing it; his agenda is purely to get a bit of recognition.

Some hecklers don't mean to be hecklers. You may be visited by the curse of a well-intentioned person who has no intention of heckling you but manages to do just that nevertheless. That is the eager beaver who seems to have a question, comment, or challenge every few minutes.

You may run into the type who loves to step on your lines. If you are telling a humorous tale, he shouts out the punch line before you reach it. But whatever you relate, he tries to anticipate the ending and beat you to it. To handle this fellow, let him give a punch line or two—the wrong punch lines. There are many stories that have two or three possible punch lines. If you know the alternative punch lines, this pest can't possibly win. You make him look foolish by giving the "right" (an alternative) punch line with an amused smile in his direction. It doesn't take more than one or two such putdowns to discourage further attempts to beat you to the snapper.

There is also the congenital skeptic who questions everything and believes in nothing: Whatever you propose or describe will bring such loud, spontaneous remarks as the following:

"Oh, that will never work."

"I tried that. It's no good."

"That old idea? Phooey."

There are no surefire cures for any of these troublemakers. One thing to do when there are too many interruptions is to halt for a moment and say something along the following lines:

Ladies and gentlemen, I welcome your questions and comments but we will be unable to cover everything if we don't curb them for a while. Give me a half-hour to explain this subject in detail, and then we will have a question and answer session or open discussion. You will all get your chance then to ask your questions and make your comments.

This usually works pretty well and enlists the aid of the audience in shushing the heckler until the half-hour is over. And then you will have—you must insist on having—control of designating who is next to speak.

Sometimes you can silence the know-it-all by asking a few questions, ostensibly in all innocence, and leading him into a cul de sac, where he admits he doesn't have the answer.

Still another technique is getting the aid of the rest of your audience in this way: When you are confronted with the wise guy or know-it-all who is simply trying to use you to gain a platform for himself or to make himself feel superior, listen to his objection or challenge attentively. Repeat his contention loudly enough for everyone else to hear it clearly. Then tell him, "Okay, you may have a good point there. Let's see what others think about this." Then turn to the rest of the audience and solicit other opinions. Others in the audience will help you squelch this guy by showing him that his is a most definite minority opinion—that he is, perhaps, a minority of one!

Being cool and collected is indispensable to all of these measures. You must appear imperturbable if you are to carry these measures off effectively. You must never allow a heckler to believe that he has "gotten to you." That is a heckler's goal, and he must be denied access to it.

HOSTILE AUDIENCES

Few audiences are hostile. They are usually seated before you voluntarily. They have come to be entertained or to gain useful information, and are thus in a receptive mood. But there are exceptions, and you can be surprised now and then by finding yourself staring at a grim-faced assemblage of frowners.

This does not necessarily mean that the audience dislikes you, nor even that they are necessarily determined to oppose whatever you plan to say to them. They may not be there entirely by choice, for example. Employers sometimes order members of the staff to attend certain seminars, symposia, or meetings, which alone may account for a marked lack of enthusiasm. You may have been preceded by a speaker they found boring or abrasive, and that can create an attitude problem. You may be facing a crowd of very young people who immediately decide you are too old to have anything to say that would interest them. Or the reverse may be true: They may be relative oldsters who wonder what they could possibly learn from a young punk and fear that you will waste their time. Or it may have nothing at all to do with you.

In fact, perhaps the term *hostile* is a bit strong. The attitude of the audience may range from indifference to distaste or mild antipathy and stop short of true hostility. Whatever it is, try to determine what the cause is. But if you cannot, carry on as though it did not exist. In most cases, the audience will warm to you after a while, if you do not bear out their fears of being a bore. Try to get the audience directly involved by asking questions, asking members of the audience to volunteer answers, inviting them to ask questions and make comments, and any other devices you can think of to actively prevent boredom. An audience will have difficulty becoming bored with a presentation in which they have become personally involved.

Unexpected Audiences

An important part of preparation is learning the identity of your audience, as I learned most painfully one day. When I am retained to present a seminar to the staff of a company or the members of an organization, I usually do whatever research is necessary to understand the interests and needs of the audience, which can vary quite a bit from one case to another. I query my client and ask for whatever literature the organization has, prior to the meeting. I often find it useful also, when I begin my presentation, to ask volunteers in the audience to tell me of their interests and why they are there, as another way of identifying my audience. But when I was asked to present a government-marketing seminar at George Washington University, I failed to do this. Instead, I assumed—a mistake in itself, of course—that it was the typical audience of small business owners eager to break into or to expand their activities in this market. Only later, reviewing the evaluation sheets, did I learn to my sorrow that the audience had included a number of government contracting officers. They had criticized me for those portions of my usual presentation on the subject which they would inevitably object to because it revealed weaknesses and flaws in the government's procurement system, as well as the need to instruct contracting officers—tactfully—in aspects of procurement too many of them do not understand. As a result, my sponsor, who had expressed approval of my presentation as he watched and listened, hastily reversed his position and never invited me to speak for him again. Had I done my job properly and learned that government contracting officers were to be in my audience, I would have sacrificed some of the more dramatic facets of my presentation and been a great deal more diplomatic about certain sensitive matters.

OTHER DISTURBANCES AND SITUATIONS

There are several other situations that you are likely to encounter from time to time during the course of making a presentation. Some of them can be rather disconcerting.

Late Arrivals

Inevitably there will be some people who don't show up, although they're scheduled, registered and paid for. But much more distracting are those who saunter in late. Every few minutes after you begin, another late arrival saunters in. It is a disturbance because it generally causes others to turn their heads to see who has arrived, and thus interferes with your continuity. Moreover, since the newcomer is late, he or she has missed your opening remarks and is going to later interrupt you with questions that would not be necessary had he or she been there on time.

I try to delay starting my presentation when I know that I am missing some attendees who are expected to be there, hoping to minimize later interruptions by late arrivals. It helps to some degree. I try also to hold back any of the truly important material from the first few minutes so that late arrivals will miss little of real substance. These two measures help a great deal. Other than that, there is little else you can do.

Late Returnees

If you are making a presentation of several hours, you will usually be giving your audience a 10-minute break about every hour and one-half. In an all-day seminar, that works out to a mid-morning and a mid-afternoon break. It is rare that you can restrict the break to that scheduled 10 minutes. Attendees customarily tarry and you must coax them back. Whether you begin promptly at the end of the 10 minutes with only about one-half your audience in their seats or wait until you get most of them back is up to you. It is a problem either way, for you will hardly ever have them all back when you start talking again. The lunch break will usually be an hour or an hour and one-half, but you will still have the problem. Half your audience will stand outside the doors of the meeting room holding a social hour while you are struggling to get started again. You may have to be a shepherd and go out to gather up your flock.

One thing that usually works is to simply begin talking when the proper time arrives, no matter how few of your audience are seated and waiting. In all fairness to those who are in their seats ready to go on, that is the right thing to do. As soon as those dawdling realize that the session has begun, they will return to their seats. What you might do to make best use of this tactic is to begin with some trivial aspect or a brief recap so that those who have been dawdling will not miss anything of importance.

Deserters

It is rare that a few people do not, one by one, get up and leave quietly before the session is over, especially in the case of an all-day seminar or workshop. It is quite disconcerting. You cannot help but wonder whether it signifies that these people are bored stiff or do not find it worthwhile to spend more time listening to your wisdom. The probable truth is that they have a travel connection to make, want to beat the rush hour, or came for certain specific information and are satisfied that they got what they came for. (On the other hand, a mass exodus from the hall before you are finished would be something to be concerned about!)

AD LIBBING AND WINGING IT

For most of us, careful preparation is a must for a successful presentation, and most of those regarded as superior speakers are usually the first to admit that thorough preparation is the secret of their success. The ability to ad lib is quite a special one, but there are numerous occasions when it is a useful and necessary skill.

Being Called on Unexpectedly

Even the most experienced and successful speakers tend to be dismayed when they are suddenly and unexpectedly called upon to rise to their feet and say a few words. (In fact, they are probably more dismayed than the less-experienced speakers; it is anathema to their convictions about preparedness for public speaking.) That, perhaps more than any other speaking situation, calls for thinking on your feet.

There are few rules for thinking on your feet. As an individual, you may or may not be able to "wing it" easily and comfortably. Most people are not that glib, and are truly at a loss for words when asked to speak extemporaneously. But there are a few hints or tips that may help.

1. If you believe that there is a slight chance that you will be called upon to speak, at least give some thought to what you might say. Even if the notion that you might be called upon has not occurred to you until you are seated at the table, it is not too late to formulate a few ideas mentally.

2. Under any and all circumstances, remain cool and calm. That's easier to say than do, but at least give the impression that you are cool and calm by using the technique explained in 3.

3. Smile and take your time rising to your feet. Think furiously, while you are stalling for time. Turn to whomever called upon you and thank him or her profusely. If there is a head table or a similar situation, take time to thank each of the others appropriately. You can use up several minutes while you do this, giving yourself a chance to gather a few thoughts. Speak briefly—almost everyone appreciates a speech in which the end is close to the beginning—smile a great deal, thank everyone, and sit down. No one will suspect your panic; they will think you a thoughtful and eloquent individual.

Stretching It

A somewhat analogous situation is one in which something has happened in a program that delays or prevents an event originally scheduled to follow your presentation. You are suddenly asked to stretch your presentation. Once again, you must ad lib in some manner. One method I find most useful in such circumstances is to offer a question-and-answer session. I find it possible to stretch that session quite a lot by inviting both questions and comments.

You might also go back over your original presentation and select some portion to elaborate on, perhaps some topic you had deliberately summarized briefly because there was not time for full development.

Shortening It

Sometimes you run into the opposite situation. For some reason, your sponsors may wish you to shorten your presentation. That may appear to be easy, but it is not always so. Your audience has been led to expect certain coverage and will probably react if they do not get it. The thing to do is shorten coverage of the topics, but do not omit any topic, especially not one specifically advertised and promised.

Overlap and Conflict

When I am one of several speakers, I know that there are two possible problems that may arise: My remarks may be redundant, duplicating remarks made earlier by another speaker, or they may be in conflict, challenging or repudiating remarks made earlier by someone else. The latter is a much more harmful effect, but I deplore the occurrence of either one. Therefore, if I am to be one of several speakers and not the first one to speak, I manage to arrive early enough to sit and listen to the earlier speakers, so that I can do something to avoid those effects. (I cannot do anything about those who follow me.)

When I was invited to be one of several speakers allotted about 30 minutes each to speak on the subject of how to write winning proposals for government contracts, I was to be the fourth speaker. I arrived early and listened to the three speakers who preceded me.

I listened with some horror as each of those speakers repeated the well-known myth that unless one has made some prior arrangements to be the favored candidate for the contract, writing a proposal is an exercise in futility. According to this myth, the notion of open competition for government contracts is false, and the solicitation of proposals a smokescreen to make it appear that there is an open and fair competition. Each speaker, having declared that proposal writing is futile, then proceeded to explain how to write an effective proposal. And no one, not even in the audience, appeared to perceive the nonsense of this paradox.

By the time I mounted the dais, the audience had heard the same story three times and was nodding. I had a problem. I was obliged to tell this audience the truth as I know it, and yet I could not attack my predecessors on the platform. I decided to say something along these lines to introduce my remarks:

> Every rule has many exceptions, and I am going to speak to the exceptions this morning—to the ways and means of overcoming the problems and doing what may not normally be possible—coming out of nowhere as a dark horse and winning the contracts that conventional wisdom says you can't win.

I then proceeded to present my view, based on my experience, which was almost diametrically opposite of what this audience had been subjected to for an hour and a half. I did so without attacking my predecessors, and was gratified to see this somnolent audience come to life and start scribbling notes furiously.

These situations, avoiding conflict and redundancy, call for thinking on your feet, but they call also for caring enough about what you are doing to do the homework of listening to the other presenters.

7

Showmanship:
Using It Effectively

**Is being a good presenter enough for you?
Or would you prefer to be a great presenter?
Showmanship can make the difference.**

UNDERSTANDING SHOWMANSHIP

When someone says of someone else, "Boy, he really has *showmanship!*" the meaning most of us infer is that "he" has an outstanding flair for making an effective presentation—an unusual ability to dramatize or otherwise make an appearance or presentation that is especially appealing and memorable far beyond the ordinary. Phineas T. Barnum, for example, was regarded as this kind of showman, creating unprecedented drama with his exhibits. So were Florenz Ziegfeld, of the Ziegfeld Follies, and Walter Winchell, with his rapid-fire, staccato delivery and exclusive news items.

Many, if not most, performers who become the stars of their fields share one feature: They have become associated with and even identified by some unique characteristic or *shtick* of some sort. For example, Groucho Marx with the grease paint mustache and eyeglasses, Jimmy Durante making an asset of an oversized nose and his "Inka Dinka Doo" ditty, Marilyn Monroe with her breathy whisper, Milton Berle and his renowned pencil, Lucille Ball with her zany antics, and George Burns with his cigar and his advanced age, to name only a handful of many. More recent has been Michael Jackson and his moon walk.

Such characteristics identify the individual and make him or her highly distinctive and thus recognizable and memorable. Sometimes a trait or shtick is used to make a character, rather than the performer, memorable, as in the case of Peter Falk and his Columbo character, with the disreputable trench coat and the character's mannerisms. There was also Marlon Brando using cotton stuffed in his cheeks to endow the "godfather" character with a distinctive feature. James Garner has made every character he has played an anti-hero. Richard Widmark launched a most successful career as a result of the insane giggle of the psychotic killer Tommy Udo, a character he created in an early screen effort. And every great comedian of old-time movies was a distinctive character—deadpan comic Buster Keaton, comedic genius Charlie Chaplin, bumbling Stan Laurel and Oliver Hardy, and extraordinarily hapless Harold Lloyd.

America's outstanding magicians have been among the great showmen of the theater: Houdini, the great escape artist, for example, shackled and hung upside down in a huge tank of water. Then the drama was heightened further by an extremely clever ancillary bit of stagecraft: Two assistants stood by with sledge hammers, ready to smash the glass of the tank should Houdini fail to free himself in time. More recently there was master illusionist David Copperfield making a huge commercial airplane "disappear" and then topping even that by making the Statue of Liberty disappear!

Showmanship is not confined to the theater, however. Department store merchant Nordstrom, with a tuxedoed pianist tinkling the keys of a grand piano on the exquisite marble floor of his magnificent department store is exhibiting another kind of showmanship. Donald Trump's Taj Mahal in Atlantic City is a bit gaudy in the opinion of many, but they are highly conscious of its existence, nevertheless. And the great arch in St. Louis, Missouri is a testimonial to that city's flair for the dramatic.

Showmanship is the ability to raise a presentation above the mundane, above, even, the status of technically good or excellent into the rarefied atmosphere of the great, the distinguished, and the memorable. It is more than mere platform pyrotechnics, however; it reflects a presentation *strategy* that usually includes some kind of identifying characteristics. It relies on and reflects such qualities as creativity, resourcefulness, and imagination. It is most often the result of careful planning, but is sometimes the fruit of spontaneous inspiration.

SHOWMANSHIP AND PRESENTATIONS

Great speakers are also great showmen and showwomen. They have a sense of the dramatic and they give *performances* when they are on the dais. They don't wait for audiences to come to them; they reach out and grab their audiences. They take command and they dominate the room with their power. Their personalities have auras that surround and envelop their audiences. They are a *presence* in the room, poised and confident, even charismatic.

Beware of Relying on Gimmicks Alone

None of this is to say that gimmicks or shticks of any kind will alone make you a great presenter, or that they are of themselves showmanship. They are aspects of showmanship, frosting on the cake. But, no matter how imaginative and clever, theatrics alone will not get you by if your presentation is otherwise lacking. It was not Jimmy Durante's nose that made him a high-paid star and a beloved personality; his talent as an entertainer did, and he had developed that talent for years before the general public had the opportunity to see him on the large and small screens. George Burns had long since learned how to caress and make close friends of his audiences before he became the beloved octogenarian and elder statesman of show biz. Jackie Gleason was a fine actor and comic, pleasing his audiences long before he became a superstar with super performances. It is no different for you, the presenter: If you deliver worthless information, even in great style, it will still be worthless information and a worthless presentation; your audiences will certainly not acclaim you for it. But if you deliver priceless information in a lifeless and stultifyingly dull presentation, it will also be a poor presentation, and your audiences will not care to hear you speak again. You need both. You need, for a good presentation, worthwhile information, properly organized and presented in a manner that keeps your audience awake, alert, interested, and ultimately satisfied. But to make it a great presentation, you must leave your audience more than merely *pleased;* you must leave your audience happy and enthusiastic, wanting more.

For the rest of this chapter we are going to probe that which helps to make a good presentation a great one via showmanship. We are going to assume that the information you have to present is what your audience wants and needs. Your job is to so present it that they not only accept the information, but they embrace it. They enjoy the experience, they will remember you and this presentation, and they would be delighted to hear you speak again.

How Long to Have Your Audience Meet You?

You have a limited time (anywhere from 30 seconds to 8 minutes, depending upon which "expert" you ask) to make friends of your audience, to prove that you are not going to put them through an ordeal of listening to an excruciatingly dull and boring presentation. Some writers have said that the typical audience wants to be your friend. Perhaps what this really means is that the audience wants the presentation to hold their interest and perhaps even be fun. If you relieve their minds about this immediately, you are off to a great start. If you take several minutes to warm up and start to establish a link of friendliness and good will with your audience, it works against you by establishing an unfavorable first impression that you must overcome. Remember that you are a stranger standing before them, an unknown quantity. You are quite likely to look out at a sea of eyes that are neither friendly nor unfriendly, but only neutral, perhaps trying to size you up, waiting for you to break the ice. A warm-up must take place, and that applies to both you and your audience— you must warm up yourself, and you must warm up your audience. Unlike the game-show host on television, you do not have a professional comic to go out there before you do and break the audience up for you so that they receive you already in a jovial mood. You have to do your own audience warm-up and by far the best time to start doing so is the first moments "on stage."

The First Second

You have probably seen the game show host come trotting out to center stage, grinning, arms extended, bubbling over with enthusiasm. You need to do something of that sort immediately after you have been introduced. Don't trot; that's for real show biz. But do stride out briskly with a large smile and a hearty, "Thank you for that fine introduction, Henry; I do appreciate it. Wonderful to be here with you today." A warm handshake before Henry leaves the dais is not out of order, either. It helps identify you to your audience as a warm and friendly fellow human being. Do be careful here, hovver; it is quite easy to overdo the heartiness so that it appears to be an act. There is no need to be insincere. In all likelihood, you are glad to be there.

Do not appear hesitant in proceeding promptly to the business at hand. That does not mean that you must leap into the breach immediately and start lecturing. You can turn from thanking your host or introducer to your audience with that warm smile and greet them. "Good morning, ladies and gentlemen." [Or whatever is appropriate to the time of day.] "I am delighted to be here with you this morning and to have the

opportunity to talk with you about . . ." [Whatever the subject is.] However, it is also perfectly all right to stand there for
a moment, before or after the "good morning" greeting, with
a broad smile and simply gaze deliberately about the room,
meeting dozens of pairs of eyes with a friendly glance before
you greet them verbally. Many speakers and other performers
use a long moment of silence before they speak; it can be most
effective. It is important that you appear at ease, however,
and that your audience recognize that the moment of silence
is deliberate and not the result of nervousness or hesitancy.
You should strive to give off an aura of what I shall call, for
lack of a better word, "positiveness," reflecting your own self-
assurance and complete confidence in what you present.

Immediate Announcements

If there has not been anything in print introducing you or if
you are one of a series of presenters on the program, it is a
good idea to make your name quite clear, especially if you
have a difficult or unusual name, and perhaps to write it on
the blackboard or flip chart.

I usually follow my introduction, my thanks to my introducer, and my greeting to the audience by explaining that I
welcome questions, comments, and/or challenges at any time,
and that I would rather pause and clear up any failure of mine
to make myself clear than to continue in confusion. I never
suggest that the audience has failed to understand me (which
might discourage individuals from asking questions they
ought to ask), but only that I may have failed to be completely
clear. You may wish to make other announcements at this
time, such as information concerning the schedule, breaks,
handouts, or other matters. If you wish all questions to be
held until you announce a question-and-answer session, this is
a good time to make it clear. If you wish to anticipate questions in advance, this is a good time to do so. For example,
instead of waiting for attendees to approach you for your card,
you may simply explain that a supply of your cards or
brochures will be available on a table at the back of the room.

This should all take place in a few minutes so that you can get on with the more important matter of your presentation.

BE A LEADER

How you handle all this delivers an important first impression. You want to appear totally confident and in command, while simultaneously accommodating and patient. This is *your* show, and you are the leader. A great presenter is always in command as the leader. Leadership is a quality shared by the great presenter, as well as the great showman or showwoman. Leadership is also a very much misunderstood quality.

To paraphrase the ancient platitude about greatness and adapt it to leadership: Some people are born leaders, some achieve leadership, and some have leadership thrust upon them. But leadership really has two aspects: It refers to a state of affairs, a state in which someone is in the position of leader. But it refers to a quality, the talent or ability of leadership, and that is quite a different matter. Being named leader is not necessarily proof of possessing the talent or capability for leadership. We'll now consider just what that capability is.

First of all, you cannot be a leader if you do not have followers. So the first and perhaps the final test of leadership is your ability to attract and keep followers. It seems equally logical that you cannot force anyone to follow you; they must do so voluntarily. The military, for example, appoints leaders. But when the test comes, usually in the stress and heat of battle, the true leaders stand out as those whom the troops choose to follow. In short, the leader is whoever manages to inspire confidence among the "troops," and persuade them to follow.

What Inspires Followers?

On the platform, you are cast inevitably in the role of leader; it is thrust upon you. If you are destined to be a great presenter, you will rise to the role and be a great leader: You will inspire that audience to believe in you, to follow you. They will follow you because you convince them that yours is the right course, the right road to take, that you dispense truth and wisdom.

Followers are inspired by whatever gives them confidence in you as a leader. They must be convinced that you are right in your judgments, that what you are doing will be successful, that the greatest security lies in following you. You must not hesitate or falter. You must be decisive, and if you have doubts you must not reveal them.

On the platform, you must present an aura of complete confidence in what you are doing and what you are saying. When you are on the platform, it doesn't matter what you think you are or what you truly are; what matters is what your audience thinks you are, how they perceive you. They must see you as being completely in charge, sure of what you are doing, exuding confidence through every pore, the epitome of positive thinking. You must make positive statements. When you get a question, answer it directly. If you don't have the answer, don't evade the question. Admit that you do not have the answer and invite the individual to leave his name and telephone number with you, promising to get the answer to him and following up as promised. Honesty, that ability to be forthright and admit that you are only human, with not the slightest suggestion of apology for it, is part of the aura. You can, in fact, make it sound absolutely noble to be able to say, with a smile, "I don't know the answer to that, but I do know where to get it. Leave me your name and mailing address, and I will get the answer to you."

Presenting that aura is part of the showmanship of great presentations, but it is not all. Following are some other important factors.

Dress

"Dress for success" is more than the title of a successful book; it is an important injunction for everyone in the business and professional world, and especially important for one who is in the public eye, as a speaker is. But it is more than a matter of dressing expensively or stylishly; it is a matter of dressing *appropriately*—in good taste for the occasion. If you are intent on having your clothes "make a statement," make that a statement of dignified professionalism as a speaker.

Showmanship for an entertainer may mean wearing a flashy outfit on stage. That is perfectly acceptable and even helpful in that milieu. But not for you. You want to focus the attention of the audience on what you are saying, not on the distraction of what you are wearing. If you wish to be taken seriously and command respect, dress quietly, in a thoroughly businesslike manner when you are on the platform. (If you like flashy, bright-colored clothes, by all means wear them—in private life, but not on the platform.) If you are less than certain about how to coordinate items (as I usually am) and have no one to advise you, you can easily play it safe: A simple solution is to wear a dark suit, dress, or skirt, a white or light-colored shirt or blouse, a simple tie, dark socks or stockings, and simple black or brown shoes. You can't go wrong with that.

Keep your pockets as empty as possible when you are on the platform. Bulging pockets destroy the tailored lines of your clothes, and noisy items jangling and clicking in your pockets as you move about are definitely distracting. I carry a briefcase with me when I speak, and I deposit it out of sight on the lectern before the audience assembles. I store all the miscellaneous stuff I might otherwise carry in my pockets—airline tickets, schedules, notes, and so on—in the briefcase until the meeting is over.

Mannerisms and Hands

The way you present and carry your person on the dais is part of showmanship. Most of us have mannerisms of some sort, often quite unconscious ones. We cross our arms without thinking about it, in what may appear to others to be a defiant gesture, whether it is so intended or not. We stroke our chin and steeple our hands when we are deep in thought. We tug our ear lobes when we are deliberating. We jangle keys or coins in our pocket when we are waiting, perhaps impatiently. And we have dozens of other such little traits, almost every one of which ought to be taboo on the platform, with one exception: they are permissible when and only when you use them deliberately to illustrate a point. Otherwise they are distracting and, to many people sitting in audiences, most annoying.

If you find yourself extremely conscious of your hands and at a loss for what to do with them, it is a definite sign that you are focusing on yourself rather than on your audience and what you want to tell them. I can't tell you what to do with your hands, for I don't know. I don't know what I do with my own hands when I speak. I am so intent on the messages I am delivering and on making sure that my audience gets my messages I don't know that I have hands, let alone what it is that I do with them. (That is the way it ought to be and will be when you reach the point where you simply forget about yourself and concentrate on your listeners.) Doing any of the many things experts will usually advise you are wrong things to do with your hands reveals nervousness; worse, it reveals amateurishness as a speaker. I can't tell you what to do with your hands, other than to let them hang down naturally at your sides but I can tell you what *not to do* with them:

- Do not stand, feet spread, and hands clasped behind you as though you are a soldier ordered to stand "at ease."
- Do not stand with your hands in your pockets.
- Do not clasp your hands before you as though they were a fig leaf.
- Do not stand with hands on hips.
- Do not conceal your hands by standing with arms folded.
- Do not stand with hands clasping your upper arms in a kind of variation of arms folded.

Posture is another problem, not unrelated to that of hands and mannerisms. Perhaps you are an habitual sloucher or a shuffler, staring at the floor when you are in private conversation and trying to think at the same time. Don't do it on the platform. Be conscious of your posture, especially if you have any bad posture habits privately. Stand relaxed but straight, gazing always at your audience, meeting their eyes. Don't clutch or lean on the lectern or any other fixture for support; let your two legs support you. Don't bounce on the balls of your feet, rock back and forth, or stand like Gibraltar in one place. Move about the platform, easily and in a businesslike manner, but don't sway, rock, or bounce in place when you are not moving about.

Style

Style is an integral part of showmanship. Every speaker has a distinctive style or is in the process of developing one. But style exists at more than one level and is marked in each case by the mannerisms, characteristics, and personality of the individual. That is, style can be described in both individual and in general terms. The following few adjectives might be applied in any given case to characterize a presentation style:

Humorous	Conversational
Humorless	Emotional
Blunt	Unemotional
Diplomatic	Analytical
Mild mannered	Enthusiastic
Aggressive	Technical
Challenging	Dramatic
Pleading	Subdued
Polemic	Laid back
Oratorical	

In most cases a given style can be characterized, perhaps even identified, by several of these terms. Your own style, for example, might be a humorous one, while it is analytical and conversational. It could also be dramatic, analytical, and aggressive. Or any of many other combinations. You might be an emotional or an emotionless speaker. You might tend to the polemic, arguing your case as though against opponents. Your style might well be oratorical, also, in that case, but it could also be dramatic and analytical.

To some degree, the content of your presentation dictates the style. When I present many of the subjects I speak on, for example, I am compelled to cite and dispel many myths about the field. I can thus hardly avoid being disputatious to some degree. That, in turn, compels me to utilize polemics, at times, and even to engage in a touch of oratory occasionally. I am often challenging and always highly enthusiastic. But I do use humor occasionally, and I do get emotional.

What this adds up to is that there is rarely any such thing as a pure style. Most speakers employ a variety of styles, according to circumstances, as well as according to their own personalities. However, there is little doubt that in most cases the dominant style is primarily a reflection of the speaker's personality, which inevitably shines through the presentation and the carefully planned remarks. Still, much of your style is the result of deliberate planning.

Actually, periodic shifts in style are beneficial, helping greatly to avoid monotony. It is easy to overdo anything, and a lengthy presentation that is pure oratory or pure polemics would soon make eyelids heavy throughout the hall. Study your subject matter and the objectives you wish to achieve, and plan your style and changes of style accordingly.

Humor

Humor is an essential part of "show biz," and so many people regard it as a necessity for all showmanship. That is not true; showmanship does not necessarily require humor at all. Contrary to popular conceptions—misconceptions, really— you do not have to be a comedian nor even a humorist to be a successful presenter. A humorous tale helps to keep an audience receptive and relaxed, but comedy is a highly skilled art, and not everyone manages to learn how to handle it well. In fact, many highly successful speakers have not one humorous story in their repertoire. However, if you insist on trying to be a poor man's Bob Hope, this section is for you.

Humor is hazardous and, with the increasing sensitivities in our society, it grows ever more hazardous. You can turn a good presentation into a total disaster with just one ill-advised story. You must be careful that your humor is not based on, characterized by, or makes reference to any of the following themes:

- Racial, national, or ethnic
- Physical or mental infirmities
- Sexist or chauvinistic
- Sexual practices

All the foregoing are almost certain to give offense to someone. Even if no one in your audience is a member of some national, racial, or ethnic group that is the butt of your story, many people find such humor in bad taste generally and are offended by it.

Guidelines for Safe Humor

The hazards of taboo humor need not limit you. Entertainer Bill Cosby is one outstanding example of an entertainer who manages to be humorous without resorting to questionable themes or devices. There are many ways to be humorous without giving anyone reason to be offended. Make yourself the butt of the humor when possible. Golf stories are abundant, funny, and "safe," as long as they skirt the danger zones. Mother-in-law stories are often okay, but they can be dangerous if they are too biting and there are mothers-in-law in your audience. The smart-alec college kid son of a hard-working, self-made man is the subject of much humor that people do not find offensive, and many of "good news and bad news" genre are funny and harmless. In general, try to stick to good-natured fun stories.

Make Your Humor Relevant

The most important point is this: If you use humor, make the stories relevant to your subject. Never introduce an irrelevant story merely to get a laugh. Use humor only to make or illustrate a point. When I enumerate several features that I consider necessary elements in a proposal, I am sometimes asked which I think are the most important. I sometimes respond to that by narrating the story of the trainee paratrooper at Fort Benning, Georgia, who asked his sergeant how many practice jumps he had to complete before qualifying for assignment to a permanent unit.

"All of them," his sergeant replied.

Learn How to Tell a Story

Some people appear to be "born" storytellers—to have an instinct for telling a story so that it draws a big laugh from everyone listening. Others seem to be never able to tell a funny story effectively. However, the right way to tell a story can be learned.

First of all, try to tailor your humor to your audience, as well as to your subject and the point you are making at the moment. If, for example, you are addressing nurses, physicians, or others of the medical profession and you want to tell a golf story, make the golfer a doctor; that always makes the story more interesting for the audience. Or if the listeners are all specialists—anesthesiologists, for example—make the golfer an anesthesiologist. But it might be even funnier to make him a plastic surgeon or a pathologist, in some cases, depending on the story. Even stories that are not particularly funny sometimes become rib-ticklers when the story is somehow linked to who or what the listeners are or to their special interests.

The humor is normally based on the ludicrous, the surprising, the irrational, the switch, or the exaggerated. And the revelation depends on the "punch line." There is a buildup and then the ridiculous and surprising revelation. If the buildup does not set the stage properly for the punch line, the story loses its humor. (This is true for even the one-liner.) The punch line delivered improperly is also a death knell for humor. Example, using Henny Youngman's most famous one liner: Wrong way: "Take my wife, please." Right way: "Take my wife—please." Without the pause, while the listener thinks you mean "Take my wife, for example," the line is not funny. It becomes funny with the switch, which is the surprise ending delivering a totally different meaning.

I find that humor works best with a large audience. The tiny titter of an individual spreads in a wave when the audience is a large one. The effect is usually much less pronounced with a small audience.

You Don't Have to "Lay Them in the Aisles"

Humor in a presentation does not have to be hilarious. It does not have to "kill" or "destroy" an audience, as comedians sometimes describe their performances when they have had an exceptionally appreciative audience. It can be wry and mildly amusing. Usually, when it is turned inward, making yourself the butt and your foibles the subject, you get that effect. When I lecture on proposal writing for government contracts, invariably the question of "wired" proposal requests is raised by someone. How many such requests, asks the audience, are wired or written so that no one except some favored contractor is likely to be able to even qualify to compete, much less win the contract. I explain that yes, it does happen that some requests for proposals are wired, but often it is quite possible to win such contracts anyway; it is very difficult for the agency to do more than give someone an edge. If another contender for the contract is aggressive, determined, and just a bit clever, he can win even the wired contract. And to prove my point I explain how I once had a request wired for me and managed very cleverly to lose the contract anyway! That always evokes a hearty guffaw, of course, while proving my point. It is far more effective—and funnier—that explaining how I won a contract that had been wired for someone else, although I generally offer one of those examples, too.

Study comedic performers carefully and practice telling stories to your friends until you master the technique. Don't hesitate to use appropriate gestures, grimaces, and dramatic pauses; they help greatly to set the mood and sharpen the comedic effect.

Your Stories Don't Have to be Funny at All

A lively and entertaining presentation usually includes a number of anecdotes, but they don't have to be humorous. There are many little stories that help greatly to put your presentation across without being humorous. But, like the humorous stories, they must be relevant and help make or illustrate your points. You may hear such stories referred to as *case histories, anecdotes, examples,* or even by other names; their usefulness is that they are interesting tales and true stories, examples of what you present.

Even though these are not intended to be humorous, one way to make such anecdotes especially interesting is to use the technique of the punch line: End the story with a switch or surprise. Sometimes I tell the tale of the brash young merchant who tried out a reckless new idea. He wouldn't listen to his competitors, who assured him that it was a foolish idea that would surely bankrupt him: He offered his customers an unconditional money-back guarantee, no questions asked. His name was Montgomery Ward, and his idea worked pretty well. The story is much more effective when the name is withheld until the end and is then released as a surprise.

Showmanship, then, is whatever makes your presentation especially attention getting, impressive, and memorable. It may be a flair for the dramatic, an ability to act out roles, or other distinguishing characteristics. Whatever it is, having it can make a major difference in your success on the platform. If you are one of the fortunate ones, it comes to you instinctively: Something about you dominates the room immediately you rise to your feet and face the audience. But if it does not, don't despair; you can do a few things to enhance your presence and make it impressive and memorable.

Always dress impeccably, wear clothes that are stylish and well-tailored, with personal grooming equally irreproachable.

Another characteristic that will make you stand out is diction: Take the time and trouble to enunciate each word distinctly, and be careful of pronunciations. Do not use any word if you are not sure of its correct pronunciation.

Know what image you wish to project, but be sure that it is one that fits you naturally and easily. Better a genuine you than a poor imitation of someone else. If you do dialects well and you can use them without giving anyone offense, use them. If you have some natural acting ability and wish to portray various roles and add drama to your presentation, that can be highly effective. If you have a good sense of comedy or satire, add the light moments to your presentation. If you have some unique or distinctive *shtick,* and it fits, use it. But always be you.

8

Presentation Strategies

Strategy is an imprecise word, but a crucial
concept that can make the difference
between brilliant success and dismal failure.

STRATEGY CAN BE A SECRET WEAPON

Strategy is a much used word and a little used idea, possibly
even a little understood idea. (Sometimes the distinction between strategy and tactics is indeed a fine one.) It is an idea
probably associated most frequently with war and military
operations, but is no less important for planning and execu-
tion of activities, such as presentations. Consider a written
proposal, for example. It can be the most important document
you have ever prepared, one on which a contract for many
dollars depends. (Government contracts awarded as a result
of competitive proposals have often run to *billions* of dollars,
in fact.) You are not alone when you pursue a large contract;
the larger the contract, the greater the number and the more
able your competitors. What makes the difference? What
causes one proposal to stand out above the others to win the
contract?

The critical factor is often strategy, and it may well be the
decisive factor. I have many times witnessed an underdog

competitor emerge as a dark horse and win the contract through the secret weapon of a superior strategy. It is not at all uncommon for upstart competitors, often newcomers in the field, to "come out of the woodwork" to win the contract. Such upsets are almost always due to superior strategic planning.

Proposals: Planned Versus Unplanned Strategies

In a sense, all proposals are based on some strategy, but the strategy is not necessarily a conscious one. That is, it may be (and should be) one that has been deliberately designed and executed or it may be one that is not the result of conscious effort but has become the strategy by default. In a typical example, each proposer studies both the request for proposals and all possible competitors most intensely. He is searching for strengths and weaknesses of his own organization and those of other vis-à-vis the contract requirements and each other. He decides that the client really needs someone who can make an unusually quick response to the need, and he finds that he happens to have a singular advantage over competitors in this case: Certain circumstances provide a special ability to do just that, to respond with extraordinary rapidity in this case. He therefore bases his proposal on that advantage, stressing it to highlight his exclusive ability to turn the job around at unusual speed and arguing the importance of this to the success of the project. His strategy, arrived at deliberately after study, is to offer to do something he believes the others will not be able to do or, at least, will not perceive as an important issue. Competitors base their proposals on their excellent overall capabilities and equally fine track record—their strategy, adopted unconsciously. Probably they don't even think of it as a strategy, but strategy it is.

Not all presentations, written or vocal, are made in sales or other directly competitive situations. You will always be competing with distracting influences vying for the attention of your audience. That does not lessen the need for presentation strategies. Remember that strategies exist at several levels, as well as in several classes and categories. Consider, for example, the many broad goals you must address in any presentation:

- Getting and keeping the attention of your audience
- Identifying—clearly—the true objective of the presentation
- Bonding with your audience
- Establishing credibility
- Being persuasive

These goals are not unrelated to each other, as will become apparent during the following discussions, but it is most helpful to identify each of these separately and think about strategies for each.

STRATEGIES FOR GETTING AND KEEPING ATTENTION

The necessity for immediately commanding the attention of your audience, whether they are listeners or readers, is beyond dispute in the sales and advertising professions. You see evidences of it every time you turn on your television and view a commercial. A wide variety of devices are used to gain your attention, including cartoons, humor, drama, satire, burlesque, and music. Some of these are so boring or bland that they fail to command any of our attention; they invite a quick trip to the refrigerator or an aside to another in the audience. Some are boring but address our wants or concerns so directly that we may watch and listen anyway. Some are so grotesquely improbable that it is their very improbability that makes them attention-demanding and memorable, for example, that familiar "ring around the collar" commercial. Some are completely banal, but so humorous that they turn into catch words, for example, "Where's the beef?" Some are intensely dramatic, such as a hospital emergency room scene or some violent event. And some are so entertaining that they become independent entertainment features, as with the "California Raisins."

The strategies may be readily apparent: They are strategies of humor, drama, horror, curiosity, fear, and self-interest. But there are substrategies (or tactics) of how to achieve these. Is humor to be sophisticated or lowbrow, that is, drawing room or bar room? Is it to be satire or slapstick? Cartoons or live actors? There are many alternative possibilities, and the alternatives exist equally in all major strategic arenas, whether you choose to use humor, drama, intrigue, mystery, surprise, or another technique.

A Few Examples

There are many ways to implement strategies. Here are two methods I have used from the platform to gain attention and to regain it if it appears to be flagging:

- I challenge my audience with the charge that I doubt that they know what business they are in. (See Chapter 5.) Not surprisingly, this rather startling statement gets immediate attention from the audience.

  The follow-up to this heightens the effect, as I then ask volunteers to describe or explain to me their businesses. The entire situation has suddenly become very personal, a contest between us.

- There are many other techniques or tactics to make an audience sit up and take notice of you. They are best introduced at the beginning of the presentation when attention appears to be flagging, or whenever you introduce a new subject. For example, in presenting a seminar on marketing, I advise an audience that I am going to show them several ways in which they can win contracts without being the low bidder. That is, I can show them how to *appear* to be the low bidders in some situations, even when they are not. In introducing the subject of proposal writing, I promise to show them how to avoid a common mistake that plagues many contractors. And in discussing doing business with the government, I promise, in advance when introducing the subject, to show them how to avoid that common problem of excruciatingly slow payment by government agencies. In fact, I promise to show them how to get paid more promptly by the government than they usually do by private-sector clients.

There is a common factor in each of these attention-getting tactics I have described: Each and every one of these devices addresses a specific problem that businesspeople have. Identify at least one "worry item"—a commonly recognized problem that most of your audience has cause to worry about, promise to discuss it and, better yet, offer solutions, and you will most certainly have their attention. (This tactic underscores the importance of knowing your audience.) You can do this one worry item at a time, or you can announce all the worry items and promised solutions in advance and refresh the audience on each one as the item arrives to discuss it. Most important, however, do not make *any* promises you cannot keep.

There is another aspect to this, one that you may recognize because it is a commonly used device in advertising and sales. Ideally, when planning a presentation (especially a sales presentation), you search for and identify good worry items. ("Good" means worry items that are of great importance to the individual, making the promise of solution a powerful motivator.) However, it is a well-established technique to manufacture worry items. That is, it is a common practice to "educate" the listener to what he or she *ought* to worry about, if that worry has not yet occurred to them independently! The "ring around the collar" television commercial is an excellent example of that, but there are many others. The security alarm business has been running television commercials lately dramatizing the problem of burglars and showing how their alarm system frightens them off, as well as sounding alarms if they are foolish enough to break in anyway.

Insurance company advertising is often based on the same technique.

Suppose that you are delivering a training seminar to an audience of salespeople. If they are inexperienced, they may not know yet what their chief worry items ought to be. But whether they are or are not experienced salespeople, they have problems that need to be solved. One way to get their attention is to introduce some common worry item of selling: What to do when the customer says no. Every salesperson would like to know more about how to handle that problem. Or how to handle the objection, "It's too expensive." Or how to get past the secretary to see the executive to whom you are trying to sell insurance.

One of the problems many small government contractors have is getting paid promptly by government agencies. I can usually get the rapt attention of an audience by reminding them of this and promising to show them how to overcome the problem. They also sit up when I promise to show them how to avoid contract disputes—after I have explained what a problem that can be if preventive steps are not taken in advance.

Everyone has concerns. Young people worry about being able to afford college. Middle-aged men may worry about job security. Smokers fear that they won't be able to quit. Whatever your presentation, you can usually find a number of relevant worry items that you plan to address, and you can parade a few of these in front of your audience.

Other Attention-Getting Strategies

Among the many other strategies and methods for commanding attention is what I call "startling statistics." These are simply numbers that impress by their magnitude or the messages they send. When I announced that the company I represented employed over 4,000 people and operated 45 offices nationwide, it commanded at least respectful attention, much more so than would a claim of being "the largest in the industry" or other unprovable generalization. Details, especially quantified ones, are far more impressive than are adjectives. Explain that over two million new mail order ventures are launched every year and not more than a few hundred survive, and you arouse some interest. Report the number of business failures, bankruptcies, AIDS cases, heart failures, divorces, foreclosures, and other such data to an audience with reason to have concerns in those areas and you command attention.

Humor is always a good means for getting attention, as long as the humor is not offensive and is relevant. You may relate the tale of the traveler who reported that he personally verified that the Concorde flew faster than sound because the stewardess slapped his face before he opened his mouth. It is humorous in any case and should not be offensive to anyone, but it should be told only if it is relevant to the subject of your presentation.

STRATEGIES FOR IDENTIFYING YOUR OBJECTIVE

It is surprising how often a presenter rambles on and on without letting the audience in on where he or she is going, that is, identifying the objective of the presentation. As a presenter, if you want to hold your audience, you must take them into your confidence and tell them where you are taking them. (It is a simple leadership principle to tell your followers where you are going together.) Doing this requires that you have yourself identified your objective in some highly specific way. Don't be confused by the fact that the subject of your presentation has been announced in advance by one means or another. Identifying your subject is not the same as identifying your objective. Your subject may be "Teen Age Pregnancy," but your objective may be "How to Avoid it" or "What to do About it." And even that may be sharpened, depending on the audience and your presentation. The objectives suggested might be suitable for an audience of teenagers or even the parents of teenagers, but it would be quite different for an audience of sociologists or government planners. It might then be "Coping with a Growing Social Problem" or "The Social Impact of Teen-Age Motherhood."

The way to arrive at this kind of specificity, if you have difficulty in doing so, is to put yourself in the listener's place: Why is he or she there? It is possible that some people attend a lecture out of simple curiosity to learn more about some subject, but it is more likely that they are there to learn something that will be of direct use. A presentation delivered to help listeners achieve a goal or solve a problem is certainly of greater interest to most people than one sounding like a high school or college lecture delivered in the name of "education."

A "how to" objective is always a good one. In general, people are always interested in learning how to do things they did not know how to do before, whether it is understanding the rules and strategies of football or methods for winning a job with a top company. "How it works" and other kinds of exposés are also good orientations. During the gasoline shortages of the late 1970s, I attended a lecture purporting to prove that the shortages and crisis were contrived by the major oil companies, the so-called "Seven Sisters," as a plot to raise prices. Whether true or not, the lecture was fascinating to all attending because the lecturer was impassioned on the subject and appeared to know what he was talking about. But, most important, it was a subject that affected all of us and puzzled many who had trouble believing that the shortage was genuine.

People rarely want knowledge for its own sake. They want to know how to solve problems and achieve goals. They want to satisfy their curiosity about subjects that affect their lives. They want to hear "the inside story" of the famous and the infamous, as a form of escapism from their own everyday existences. In cases such as the lecture just referred to, they enjoy having their suspicions confirmed by the "inside story." Or they want the vicarious thrill or pleasure of hearing the exploits of some heroic character.

STRATEGIES FOR BONDING
WITH YOUR AUDIENCE

Bonding, as a term applied to human relationships, has come more and more into vogue in recent times. Ordinarily we speak of male bonding, female bonding, parental bonding, or establishing a close relationship with another person or group of people. The idea may be applied to your relationships with an audience, too.

Bonding with an audience means establishing a warm and close relationship with them. For many, it seems to be a natural talent. Bob Hope, Dean Martin, Ronald Reagan, and Johnny Carson, to name only a few, seem to have this instinctive ability to radiate warmth and good fellowship, and are almost instantly likable personalities. General and President Dwight Eisenhower, affectionately known as "Ike," had that kind of persona, too: He was more than a war hero to millions of Americans. On the other hand, another towering military figure, General Douglas MacArthur, projected a totally different persona, one of autocratic and aristocratic dominance, a man to be respected for his unquestionable military brilliance and peerless record, but not, perhaps, to be instantly liked.

Perhaps one difference is that those first named genuinely like people, and that liking shows when they are before an audience. It is hard not to feel a bond with someone who shows that kind of warmth. On the other hand, it takes a great deal longer to "warm up" to someone who is reticent and retiring. Shyness is not a characteristic that will help you establish a warm bond with your audience. Yet, brashness is not a helpful trait, either. What is necessary is to show your liking for the people seated before you. Here are a few suggestions for doing that:

- Show complete respect for your listeners by not only inviting their questions and comments, but by hearing individuals out—listen attentively and patiently—and giving his or her remarks serious consideration before responding.

- Make it clear that you are completely relaxed on the platform, that is, you know that you are among friends. A relaxed posture on your part helps create a relaxed atmosphere that the audience can enjoy with you.

- Don't appear to be hurried in your presentation. Smile and pause frequently, especially when you make a point that might be controversial, deliberately giving the listeners a few moments to absorb what you have just said and react—vocally—if they wish to.

- Be careful that you do not embarrass anyone, as you might do if someone asks a "dumb question," and you do not think before answering. The rest of your audience may laugh, but they will feel less relaxed and friendly in your presence. If anyone is to be the butt of humor, it must be you.

- Don't appear to "believe your own press clippings"— that is, don't be overly impressed with yourself. You may get a flowery introduction, but if it is somewhat excessive in its praise, dismiss the excess with some mildly self-deprecatory remark. (Motion Picture Association official Jack Valenti handled this by remarking that if he had known he was to be so eulogized he would have had the decency to die first.) However you handle this, present a reasonable degree of modesty and humility to offset any excesses of an eloquent introduction.

- If yours is an extended session that requires breaks, you will almost surely be approached during breaks by individuals who want to ask questions on a somewhat personal basis or otherwise wish to meet you personally. Accord them complete courtesy.

Practice these methods and work at overcoming any shyness or reticence that is inherent in you. The results may surprise you.

STRATEGIES FOR ESTABLISHING CREDIBILITY

Believability was discussed briefly in Chapter 3, primarily with respect to marketing presentations. However, credibility is a necessary element of every presentation. There is not much point in delivering a presentation of any kind if your audience does not place any credence in what you say.

Certain factors that affect credibility are related to some of the matters discussed earlier in this chapter; for example, stating the objective or promises made in connection with stating the objective. Ask yourself first whether any promise you make appears to be too good to be true? Not that appearing to be too good to be true invalidates the promise automatically; it does not. It does, however, require more proof than a less extreme promise would. Those gurus of real estate riches who promise to teach you how to acquire wealth without investment in real estate ventures work hard at "proving" their claims with testimonials and what appears to be logic and inside information about subjects; for example, financing, mortgages, property transfer, and government loans and grants, that are quite mysterious to most of us. They deliver such information—and perhaps some misinformation along with it, in this case—with great confidence and in a totally self-assured manner. That alone greatly assists in achieving credibility. Certainly you must show complete faith in what you are saying; you must make your statements in a quite positive manner; and you must respond to questions and challenges with equally calm aplomb.

This takes advantage of the psychological side of being believable: It is much easier to appear credible to someone who has a direct and selfish reason to want to believe what you are saying. A confident air is always helpful, and may be the only "proof" needed when the audience has a direct interest—something desirable to gain—in believing what you say. Moreover, an audience with something to gain by believing you will usually accept as logical proof data that they might not otherwise accept.

Aside from taking advantage of people's hopes and fears, there are other less subjective factors that will help you to achieve credibility:

- Your expertise should be established as early as possible, to create that favorable initial impression as someone who knows what he or she is talking about. That begins with your introduction. You should write your own introduction, if at all possible. (Those introducing you to an audience are usually quite pleased to get your own statement of what you think the audience ought to know about you.) This is no place for false modesty. Lay out all the credentials that are relevant to your presentation and your qualifications to speak on the subject. You can blush modestly and wave it all aside immediately after your introducer states it all, but be sure the audience knows who you are.

- Name dropping is of itself not an admirable practice, but there is no reason to refrain from using illustrative anecdotes, from time to time, to reinforce your qualifications. You can do so and still appear to be suitably modest. For example, when I refer to some outstanding proposal success, even if it was one I wrote alone, I always refer to "we," suggesting that it was a team effort. In some cases, I do not even confess to having been part of the effort, but refer to "they" as a former client or a case study I learned of indirectly. I thus manage to avoid using the perpendicular pronoun excessively often, while still reinforcing my representations of expertise and authority.

- Anyone can generalize about almost anything, from how to build a house to how to win an election or cure a disease. Generalization is no proof of worthwhile knowledge, but, in addition, is suggestive of dilettantism or deliberate efforts to bluff your way through. It can thus thoroughly destroy credibility.

  The opposite side of that coin is specificity and detail. The ability to supply detailed and highly specific information is always convincing of authority. It means that you are either a true expert in the subject, with appropriate breadth and depth of knowledge, or that you have done your homework and are properly prepared to deliver a credible and convincing presentation.

- It should hardly be necessary to point out here that accuracy is essential to being credible. The specific details prove your authority only if they are accurate. It is far better to be honest, if you are not sure of some point, and admit that you can't recall the exact figure or, if you are knowingly offering a rough estimate, say so. Otherwise, by the most perverse of Murphy's laws, there will always be someone in the audience who happens to know the exact amount and who will immediately embarrass you with it. Bluffing is always a high-risk venture, and eating your words is never a joy. Incidentally, I have found it face-saving, in many cases, to be able to direct my audience to a source for more detailed information when I could not recall it or did not know it. Usually, citing a source of further detail results in immediate scribbling of notes by most of the audience, testifying to the satisfaction with that response to a question.

THE STRATEGIES OF PERSUASION

Persuasion is a direct dependent of credibility. Still, despite the relationship, they are distinctly different entities. You may achieve credibility without achieving persuasion. An audience may believe what you have presented and yet be unmotivated to do as you suggest. However, you are most unlikely to be persuasive without first being highly credible.

In fact, we are talking about persuasion in two different modes. We just discussed persuasion to believe—achieving credibility. But there is also the matter of persuasion to act, to do something you suggest, whether it is to buy something you are selling, to give up cigarettes, or to take skiing lessons.

People are persuaded to do things for much the same reason that they are persuaded to believe things. The most effective motivators are always those of self-interest: What do I gain by doing it? What do I lose or risk by not doing it?

Here again credibility and persuasion cross paths: Credibility means convincing the individual that he or she will gain, lose, or risk whatever it was you promised as a result if they did or failed to do what you proposed.

PERCEPTIONS

One important idea to bear in mind at all times is that your perception of reality in any of these or other matters is not always the same as the listener's perception. If something already appears one way to the listener, you may consider it to be unfair bias or prejudice, but it is reality to that individual. Trying to change that individual's perception is inevitably an uphill struggle. Even when you win such a struggle, the victory is usually a mixed one. As an experienced merchant put it, "Win an argument and lose a customer." Or to paraphrase, "Win the argument and lose your audience."

Given that it is probably ruinous to your presentation to enter into a battle of wits or a polemic exercise with your audience, you have two options: Either avoid controversial subjects in general, such as those that will be discussed in the next chapter, or accept the listeners' realities and work with them as best you can. That is, it is far better to try to adapt and adjust your presentation to fit the listeners' realities as much as possible.

Conventional wisdom for a salesperson encountering a strong objection from a prospective customer is to use the "yes, but" response, agreeing with what the prospect says, but pointing out some counterbalancing fact. If the prospect says your coffeemaker is more expensive than the leading brand is, you say, "Yes, it is indeed, but look at what you get for the money," then proceed to list the advantages of the high-priced coffeemaker.

In lecturing on marketing to the government, I run into the myth that all government contracts are "wired" and won only by those with "the right connections." I admit the truth that many of the truly large government procurements are subject to political maneuverings and influence, but emphasize that this is not true of the average or smaller contracts, although even there occasionally some agency does try to favor a given supplier. I rarely have trouble convincing my audience that what I say is true because I don't challenge their basic prejudice. (The fact is that U.S. government purchasing is plagued with the bungling and inefficiencies that are characteristic of all large bureaucracies, but is much cleaner, on balance, than that of most other governments.) I back up my assertions with case histories of irregular procurements and how they were either quite easily revealed as such or, more important, how a clever bidder has been able to "unwire" them. I even tell a humorous story of how I bungled a contract virtually wired for me. (See Chapter 7.)

If you present the same material to many audiences, you will probably come to know what the typical myths, biases, and misconceptions are. Still, no matter how often you deliver a set presentation to what you believe is the same kind of audience, you get a few surprises. It is thus wise to be attentive to audience reactions and try to perceive any unexpected biases or contrary opinions. One of the advantages of inviting spontaneous questions, comments, and challenges is that they reveal such problems and help you avoid painting yourself into corners.

Of course, a given audience is never completely homogeneous. Given an audience of 40 people, you may encounter as many as 40 different and even conflicting opinions, prejudices, and notions. So you must be alert for the ideas and attitudes of individuals, which may or may not reflect a majority opinion in that audience. It is important to avoid anything that arouses strong moral opposition, indignation or outrage. You'll find this especially true in an audience's reaction to the stories you tell, especially the humorous stories. Here you must be especially careful.

9

The Truth about Using Humor

Many speakers mistakenly believe that to be great speakers they must be highly accomplished comedians on the platform, and they strain mightily to achieve that status, usually unaware of the hazards it entails.

THE FALLACY OF THE POOR-MAN'S BOB HOPE

Far too many inept comic efforts are perpetrated every day on the lecture platform by good speakers who are poor comedians and not much better humorists. Yes, there is a difference between the two. At least one difference is that it is much more difficult to be a successful comedian than to be a successful humorist. But there is a more basic difference in my own view and therefore in how I shall regard and treat the subject of humor on the platform.

The Comedian Versus the Humorist

A comedian is someone whose business or main objective is humor itself. His or her sole objective is to inspire laughter from an audience. Many speakers also tell funny stories to relax their audiences with hearty laughter. Or perhaps the speaker's goal is simply to evoke the sign of success and approval represented by the laughter. Logically, a funny story told by a speaker must be meaningfully related to or illustrative of the subject of the presentation, but frequently the relationship is rather strained and somewhat tenuous. Still, like the full-time professional comedian, this kind of speaker tends to judge his or her appeal and success at least partially by how much laughter the presentation produced, as well as by the amount and heartiness of the applause at its conclusion. (But have you ever wondered whether final applause represented approval of the meat of the presentation, appreciation for the entertainment provided by the funny stories, or gratitude because the ordeal of the lecture is over?)

A Closer Look at the Humorist

A humorist is someone who exposes amusing aspects of everyday activity, primarily in human foibles and incongruous inconsistencies. The late Will Rogers fit this description rather well, getting most of his humorous ideas from incongruities he found in the daily newspaper. In fact, one of his most often repeated and best remembered lines was his introductory, "All I know is just what I read in the papers."

The humor of those I regard as humorists, rather than comedians, is most often characterized by wry remarks, such as Will Rogers' "More men have been elected between sundown and sunup than were ever elected between sunup and sundown." Or Winston Churchill's "A fanatic is one who can't change his mind and won't change the subject." Those are witty observations rather than humorous anecdotes, however. They rarely provoke belly laughs and are not intended to. They are intended to provoke appreciative chuckles and, quite often, to expose by humor the absurdity of many truths in our daily lives. Satire is a favorite tool of humorists, who use irony, parody, and even burlesque to make their points. The satire may be quite gentle, or it may be quite sharp, lampooning some individual, office, or institution. Political cartoonists, publishing their daily cartoons in newspapers and other periodicals, often use their talents to mount attacks in this manner.

The distinction between the comedian and the humorist is not always easy to make. Admittedly, my own distinction is quite arbitrary, but for good purpose: to help you avoid the dangers of trying to be a true comedian and show you how to use humor safely and effectively in your presentations. But it is not always easy to make the distinction.

True humorists are rarely serious or somber in making their presentations, and yet they have a serious purpose: They have messages to deliver, but they deliver them in a serio-comic guise, often as satire. One master of that genre is Art Buchwald, who does several newspaper columns a week, a book of his columns every few years, and speaking engagements as he wishes to. Buchwald's approach is parody, a comedic approach reminiscent of the logical aberration known as *reductio ad absurdum*—a logical fault resulting from taking some apparently valid argument to an extreme that exposes its absurdity.

Bill Cosby strikes me as much more the humorist than the comedian, although his career and professional world is strictly that of showbiz. He finds his subjects in the most mundane aspects of daily life, using satire for the most part. Johnny Carson, in the opening minutes of his nightly appearances, also turns to this brand of humor, generally based on current news events, with a great deal of success.

Many professional speakers are full-time humorists—their entire presentations are devoted to a humorous presentation, although they usually have an underlying serious intent. That underlying intent—to be a speaker who is a humorist, rather than a comedian per se—is the difference between the professional speaker and the professional entertainer. It is also the difference between the public speaking circuit and the entertainment/show-biz capital, Hollywood. Many, perhaps most, entertainers are itinerants during their early

years, as are full-time speakers. But the successful entertainer may eventually land in Hollywood or Las Vegas and do
little traveling thereafter, whereas the successful speaker
continues to be an itinerant. It is the nature of the full-time
speaking profession.

WHO ARE THE PROFESSIONAL SPEAKERS?

Not all professional speakers are full-time speakers. That is,
many professional speakers divide their time between speaking and other activities, such as consulting and writing. Dottie
Walters, for example, publishes a bimonthly magazine for
speakers and consultants and operates a busy speakers bureau, but finds time to go on extended speaking tours and even
to author or co-author an occasional book. Howard Shenson,
often referred to as the "consultant's consultant," consults,
publishes a newsletter and other publications for consultants,
writes books on the subject, and conducts many training seminars for consultants and aspirants to consulting. Many who
are in the public eye—such as journalists, authors, athletes,
scientists, public officials (elected or appointed), lawyers, doc-
tors, military officers, and sundry other kinds of careerists—
regularly speak professionally.

ACCEPTING THE INEVITABLE

Many who instruct others in the art of public speaking (I
include myself here) believe that most speakers should not
attempt to tell jokes, although they should learn how to relate
anecdotes that may or may not be amusing. First of all, most
people do not tell jokes very well. It is an art. Some people
seem to have been born with the ability to tell jokes well;
some learn to do so. But a great many never master the art at
all, and do not seem to understand that while the folks at the
office laugh at their quips and funny stories, audiences of
strangers are likely to be less charitable and less receptive to

any but skillfully told humorous stories and quips. (One of Jimmy Durante's standard pieces of business was to flap his arms in outrage and mutter in disgust, "Everybody wantsa get inta duh act." He was thus mirroring the often-expressed "Everybody wants to be a comedian" cliche of show biz.) The folks at the office or in the cocktail lounge are friends and possibly relatives and all are in a relaxed atmosphere that is much more conducive to laughter than is a lecture hall. Some speakers are misled by their success at dinner table conversations and deceived into believing that they have joined the ranks of the world's great raconteurs.

Despite the fallacy of such beliefs and despite the risks, many speakers press on with their efforts to improve their presentations by acquiring and telling a library of funny stories. Probably most speakers use comedy or humor at least occasionally in their presentations. Accepting the inevitability that most speakers will ignore any advice to be extremely bearish about using jokes, I hope in this chapter to (1) help you understand the basis for humor and become a qualified raconteur; and (2) persuade you to proceed cautiously and try to become more the humorist than the comedian.

Telling a funny story effectively is, however, a useful art and the rest of this chapter is devoted and dedicated to accomplishing just that.

THE NATURE OF HUMOR

There are comics and there are comedians, and they are defined in the entertainment world a bit differently—on a more discriminating basis—than they are in dictionaries. In this special jargon, a comedian is one whose principal act is telling funny stories and making quips. Comedians may wear funny hats or make a few gestures and faces, but their main stock in trade is a litany of jokes and quips. Comics tend to rely on "sight gags," humor that is dependent on some visual devices—props—more than on vocal humor. (Harpo Marx, for example, never spoke at all in his performances.) As a speaker, you will not be using that brand of humor, although that does not entirely rule out using a few gestures and "making faces" of surprise, astonishment, shock, and other illustrative reactions.

What strikes one individual as funny may not amuse another. Nor does the same thing amuse us each time; moods apparently have a great deal to do with it. Comedians who make a serious study of humor do believe in certain basic principles. One is surprise: The final twist or snapper must be unexpected and unanticipated. Another is incongruity: we tend to laugh at the incongruous. We also tend to laugh at others' misfortunes and at their ineptness and stupidity, as millions did at Laurel and Hardy, the Three Stooges, and other comics of that type in situation comedies.

Many of these comedic devices are unsuitable for the platform where a measure of dignity is a must. In fact, for the platform the humor must be entirely vocal, although it may be supported by grimaces and gestures that are not too undignified or in bad taste. Still, the "rules" apply: The basic ingredients are the need for an effective snapper or punch line, which must come as a surprise and be based on some incongruity.

Even so, the secret of success in being humorous is not that simple or that mechanical. There are other considerations that deal with the delivery or art of story telling: timing, buildup, and enhancements, such as the right accent or dialect, and sometimes the subtle gesture—a raised eyebrow, a look of surprise, or similar grimaces and gestures.

SOME TIPS ON STORY TELLING

A funny story, or a joke, follows the general pattern for all narrations: It has the three elements of beginning, middle, and ending or introduction, buildup, and snapper or punch line. The two critical factors are the buildup and the punch line, but timing is also of great importance.

The Elements of the Story

One reason it is so difficult to make an orderly analysis of humor is that there are so many things that evoke mirth. It is almost impossible to identify rules or principles that do not have many exceptions, but here are some general guidelines:

Telling a humorous anecdote successfully often depends on the buildup, sometimes called the setup because its purpose is to set the scene and to set up the audience for the surprise that is the punch line. For example, here are the introduction, the buildup or setup to a story, and the punch line, indicated by the numbers (1), (2), and (3), respectively:

1. That reminds me of a fellow I know who got a call at his office that he had won the state lottery. As soon as he recovered from the shock, he called his wife with the news.
2. "Listen, hon, you won't believe this but I won the lottery. Yes, forty million bucks. Can you believe it? Now, listen, I'll be coming home a little early, as soon as I straighten things out here and pick up the check. I want you to start packing immediately."

   "What shall I pack, dear? Where are we going," asked his wife.
3. "You can go wherever you want, hon, as long as you are gone when I get home," responded the happy new millionaire.

In this case, the punch line is totally unexpected. But the punch line can be less a startling surprise than a stinging retort and still be funny, as in the following example:

1. I had a friend whose wife was the spoiled brat of a wealthy mother.
2. He wasn't very successful yet, and his wealthy mother-in-law had bought her daughter and son-in-law almost everything they had to help them get started in

life. She was careful to never let her son-in-law forget it. One day they got into a squabble over what they were going to watch on the television.

"Listen you worthless nothing," said the mother-in-law. "We'll watch what I want to watch. If it wasn't for my money, this television wouldn't be here. In fact, if it wasn't for my money, even this house wouldn't be here."

3. "Yeah," said the son-in-law, "and if it wasn't for your money, *I* wouldn't be here!"

Note how (1), the introduction, sets the stage as briefly as possible. The buildup develops the scene and creates the mood, preparing the listener for a surprise twist. The punch line is then delivered in as swift and surprising a way as possible.

Each element is important to a story. However, the buildup is a most important part of the process. If you can make it a bit dramatic, getting the audience truly involved to a point where they begin to care about the outcome, the reaction to the punch line is greatly amplified. However, one way many people kill a story is by rushing through the buildup without giving the audience enough time to begin caring about the outcome and waiting impatiently for it. The other way to kill a story is by drawing out the buildup excessively. It is necessary to judge the correct compromise between the two extremes.

Some audiences will appreciate certain humor more than others. Although all audiences will be at least mildly amused by the following brief anecdote, probably an audience of young career women would be especially appreciative:

A young boy who was an excellent student was forced to admit to his father that he lost a hard-fought spelling bee in his class to a young girl who was just a bit better.

"You lost out to a mere girl?" his father demanded, a bit bellicosely.

"Dad," remonstrated the youngster, "girls aren't so 'mere' anymore."

One Liners and Quips

Quips or one liners contain all the elements in a single sentence. One of the most surefire laugh getters from Henny Youngman's one liner arsenal is, "Take my wife—please." It is delivered at a time and in a context that makes it easy for the audience to fill in the implied words "for example." The audience assumes that Youngman means "Take my wife, for example," and so is generally stunned for a brief moment, until they "get it." That an audience is deliberately misled in this manner—persuaded to expect one thing and then surprised with another—is why the punch line is also called "the switch."

This is an example of what some call a "time joke," referring to the fact that the laugh is usually not instantaneous when the punch line is delivered because the audience is taken by such utter surprise that it takes a moment for them to "catch on" to the humor. This is probably especially true for one-liners, including one that announces the postponement of a meeting of psychics due to *unforeseen* circumstances.

Timing

Timing is important to humor, and one of the factors about timing that more than one professional comedian has advocated is waiting for the laugh. Neophytes tend to expect immediate laughter after delivering the snapper, and when they don't get that reaction, they often hurry on, thereby killing their own point.

Many audiences need a few seconds to decide to laugh—to "get it" or understand and appreciate the humor. Jack Benny was considered a master of comedy timing. He would utter the snapper and then wait patiently in silence for as long as it took until the audience decided to laugh. (Of course, his facial expressions and gestures helped also.) Laughter is infectious, and many people in an audience wait for someone else to lead the way, to begin laughing. Note how often laughter begins, after a brief pause, as a giggle by one or two people and then begins to swell until the entire audience is laughing.

Some highly successful comedians deliver their material in rapid fire manner, hardly pausing between stories and quips (once again demonstrating the difficulty in understanding and explaining what humor is). This kind of delivery uses material up at a high rate and requires a large repertoire.

I have noticed the great difference that the size of the audience can make in how a story is received. A story that brings little more than amused grins and a tiny giggle from a small audience often produces belly laughs from a large audience. It is part of the same phenomenon of the contagiousness of laughter. My stories almost always go over much better with a large audience, and yours probably will too, if you don't rush the punch line. Give the audience time to get it.

Timing is also critical in delivering the buildup, which must be long enough to set the stage properly, but not so long as to weary the listener or give the punch line away. Judging this is an art form; the great story tellers cannot explain how they do it on any rational basis. However, those who stretch the buildup out at great length usually embellish it along the way with many grimaces, gestures, and asides, producing a great many incidental laughs and chuckles before they get to the big punch line. Simply pausing at certain critical points and perhaps exhibiting a certain kind of significant facial expression can build the anticipation. Tell the story with obvious relish and enthusiasm. It is difficult to persuade an audience to be enthusiastic about that which does not appear to be very important to you.

Timeliness

Some humor is timeless; it is funny whenever told. But some is dependent on when and in what connection it is sprung on an audience. Timeliness can make an anecdote funny, but the lack of it can also kill a good story. Stories that are based on events and conditions of 30 or 40 years ago might work very well with an audience of senior citizens, but it will almost surely bomb with a young audience. A quip of some 30 plus years ago was, "Think how terrible it would be if Sherman Adams died and Ike became President," referred to the fact that Eisenhower often seemed to be doing little but golfing, while his chief of staff, Sherman Adams, was very much in evidence. The story is dangerous anyway because Eisenhower admirers might be offended by it, but the point is that a youthful audience wouldn't get it at all. A less offensive politically-oriented quip—one not dependent on timeliness—is the remark generally attributed to Alben Barkley (Vice President of the United States 1949–1953) that there were two brothers, one of whom went to sea and the other of whom became Vice President of the United States. Neither was ever heard from again.

Certain humor is seasonal, especially that with holiday connotations. In the Christmas season, with the focus on shopping, a story about someone who got arrested for doing his Christmas shopping too early—he was in the store before it opened—is funnier than it would be at other times of the year. "Shopping too early" has a special meaning at Christmas time that it does not have at any other time of the year. We associate Thanksgiving with turkey, and so jokes revolving around turkey have special meaning at Thanksgiving season. Summertime is the best time to present anecdotes about vacations and vacation mishaps, as winter is the time to tell jokes about skiing.

Sardonic Observations

Observations of fact, such as dogmatic assertions by those who appear to be authorities, are often inherently and sardonically humorous with no embellishment whatsoever required. They are not always evocative of belly laughs, but they do amuse audiences, while they are often useful to constitute sharp observations, to underline or otherwise punctuate points you wish to make. Examples of these are so abundant that some can be found to fit virtually any situation. Here are just a few:

- Charles Duell, Commissioner of the U.S. Patent Office in 1899, proposed to abolish his office since, he said, "Everything that can be invented has been invented."

- Erasmus Wilson, professor at Oxford, said in 1878 that when the Paris Exposition closed, ". . . electric light will close with it and no more will be heard of it."

- In 1876, Western Union rejected Alexander Graham Bell's offer to sell his telephone patent for $100,000.

- Ironically, Thomas Watson, founder of IBM, said as recently as 1943 that he foresaw a world market for about only about five computers. Even later, in 1957, the Prentice-Hall editor in charge of business books saw data processing as a short-lived fad.

- Admiral William Leahy advised President Harry Truman in 1945 that he spoke as an expert on explosives when he said that the new atomic bomb will never "go off."

- Lewis Douglas, the U.S. Budget Director, announced the "end of Western civilization" as the result of the U.S. government abandoning the gold standard in 1933.

- Horace Greeley announced in April, 1864 in the *New York Tribune*, of which he was editor, that Abraham Lincoln was already beaten and could not possibly be reelected. (The subsequent electoral college vote was 212 to 21 for Lincoln.)

- Chester Carlson had great difficulty selling his new invention, failing to interest IBM or others to whom he offered it, until tiny Halide Corporation became interested, little dreaming that they would one day become giant Xerox Corporation as a result.

IN SUMMARY

Probably the wisest course for you to follow as a presenter is to proceed cautiously with humor. One-liner quips are generally free of hazards, as far as failure to be funny is concerned because they are such transient efforts that you can press on swiftly if the quip fails to bring a reaction. Other than that, do use relevant anecdotes to illustrate your points, preferably humorous and true ones or case histories; they are extremely useful to add interest to any presentation. Where you use anecdotes that are not humorous, try to present them in a way that produces amusement. It is often possible to structure the way you present material to make it somewhat humorous when it was not originally a humorous tale. Study the anecdote to find the item that could become a punch line. The story told in Chapter 7 of how I lost a contract that was wired for me is one example of how to structure an anecdote to play it for laughs, as well as for illustration. But there are many ways to do this. I have gotten amused reactions in advising audiences how to benefit from asking "dumb questions," as another example, illustrating by anecdote how this may be done profitably. I have gotten a great amused response in appreciation to a question I fling to an audience as a challenge and then answer for myself, as another technique that works well. Here is the typical scenario:

"How many of you use testimonial letters in your proposals? (A typical small show of hands.)

"How many of you *have* testimonial letters from your customers? (Again a small show of hands.)

"What's wrong with the rest of you? Why don't you all have many testimonial letters for your good work?" (No response; I pause only briefly.)

"I will tell you why you don't have those testimonial letters: You don't *ask* for them!"

I wait for the inevitable laugh and then go on to lecture my audience on how to get and use those testimonial letters. It has proved to be most effective to scold my audience, with obvious good humor and obviously feigned aggressiveness. We then have a good laugh together, and they remember the message.

10

Guidelines for Speech Writing

"It takes three weeks to prepare a good ad lib speech."
—Mark Twain

WHY THE NEED FOR SPEECHWRITING GUIDELINES?

Whether the speechmaker's groan, when requested to deliver a speech, is louder than the audience's groan when notified that there will be one, speeches almost invariably produce symptoms of apprehension and unhappiness. Unfortunately, the apprehension and unhappiness are all too often well-founded: We have all suffered through far too many stumbling, rambling, cliche ridden, platitudinous orations and too few entertaining and enjoyable ones.

It doesn't have to be this way—and shouldn't be when the speech maker has time to prepare. In the military I was taught that if there is one unpardonable sin in a military operation, it is being taken by surprise—being unprepared. The late Polish statesman, composer, and celebrated concert pianist, Ignace Jan Paderewski, was reported to have had the following to say about his own preparation for his many concert appearances: "When I miss practice for one day, I know it. When I miss practice for two days, my teacher knows it. And when I miss practice for three days, my audience knows it." Speech making is not unlike this. The quality of your presentation is inevitably in proportion to the amount and quality of your preparation. When you are properly prepared, neither you nor your audience need suffer. In fact, you will both enjoy the experience.

Here the analogy with concert appearances ends, however, for preparation for speechmaking is more than rehearsal, much more (although rehearsal plays a part). It is also and even more significantly preparing the material to rehearse: Writing the speech.

A speech is one special kind of presentation, although there are many kinds of speeches you might be called on to make—for awards, tributes, graduations, bar mitzvahs, weddings, eulogies, invocations, commencements, retirements, anniversaries, keynote addresses, and for other occasions. Even when the experienced, highly skilled speaker makes such addresses, it is usually evident whether the speech was carefully prepared, hurriedly improvised, or spontaneous; rare is the individual who can make a good impromptu speech. However, with the right preparation—speechwriting—anyone can be a success as a speechmaker.

WRITING A GOOD SPEECH

One reason people write poorly is that they begin to write too soon, before they are ready to write. That is, they start writing before they have thought things out, completed initial research, drafted an outline, and made notes, before they have made themselves even marginally expert in what they choose to write about. James Michener is an excellent model to follow: He writes great novels—after two years of research for each. You need not spend two years, but most successful writers, whether they are writing a novel, a play, a nonfiction book, a user's manual, or a speech, spend at least as much time preparing to write as in writing. They research and study all aspects of their subject until they have become at least marginal experts in the subject. In some respects, what you read or hear is the tip of the iceberg: The writer has sifted through tons of information to extract and refine the few ounces of essence he or she wants to offer you. And then he or she polishes those few ounces repeatedly until they shine with full brilliance.

The following is an outline of steps to developing a good speech. Note the amount of activity in preparing to write before putting pen to paper or pressing the first key on the keyboard.

1. *Define your subject generally*—Child care, marketing, environmental pollution, the school system, or whatever is to be your general subject.

2. *Focus on your specific subject*—A specialized area of the general subject—problems with teenagers, what you can do about pollution of the environment, how to work for a better school system, or other specific topic.

3. *Define your goal*—What is it you want to accomplish —promote a plan, arouse the rabble, organize a group, extol someone's virtues, or run for office?

4. *Do your initial research*—Use your own knowledge, the library, local government facilities, radio and television stations, personal interviews, other resources to gather information.

5. *Consider surrounding factors*—When (time of day, day of week, season) and where (school, lecture hall, meeting room, outdoors) you are to speak; the audience (common characteristics and expectations); and your natural speaking style, if any (humorous, serious, aggressive, retiring).

6. *Draft an outline, with traditional three subdivisions* —Introduction, Body, Conclusion.

7. *Draft the speech*—Follow the outline and write a first draft of the speech.

8. *Second draft*—Edit the first draft and do more research, if and as necessary; it is not an uncommon need. Revise the outline, too, if your draft writing indicates that the outline is not totally right. That need is also not at all uncommon.

9. *Additional drafts/final draft*—Unless you are an unusually good writer, your speech will require or at least benefit from as many revisions as you can manage to make. Keep reviewing your manuscript critically and revising it until you are satisfied or have run out of time.

10. *Revising the introduction*—The introduction is the last thing to write. However, it is a necessity psychologically for many writers (I am one) to have drafted an introduction as a first step, although with the consciousness that it is a dummy introduction that you will scrap later. You will write the final introduction after you have written the final draft of the body of the speech, and know precisely what you are introducing.

11. *Revising the finish*—A speech needs lots of material in the middle, but it should also have a great finish.

Now let us look at these steps more closely and consider the specific details of how to carry them out effectively.

DEFINING THE SUBJECT

You may be asked to speak on some given subject, although you always choose your own specific material, or the subject may be left to you, but the general common interest of the audience is clearly implied. If a small-business group invites me to speak to them and leaves the choice of subject to me, I am not going to discuss meteorology or playwriting. I will ask myself what this audience wishes to hear. If the program chairman insists that the topic is left to my own choice, one thing I can do is to ask what some recent speakers have talked about. Another way is to ask in what kinds of businesses are the members of the audience typically engaged. Another is to ask for samples of literature or newsletters the organization publishes. Still another way is to make up a sizable list of possible topics and submit them to the program chairman for reactions and suggestions.

Note that this is oriented to helping you find out what the listeners are most likely to be interested in and most likely to want to hear and discuss. No subject is a good one unless the audience is interested in it.

I use still another approach, when none of the ones suggested appear to be working for me. And even when they are, this is a good "insurance policy" for a speaker: I prepare a great deal more information than I can use, and I edit and cut spontaneously, as I speak and perceive the interests of the audience.

If you choose a topic about which you already know a great deal, you will not have to work as hard as if you had chosen one that you knew nothing about, and the speech will probably go better, nevertheless. With a bit of imagination, you can usually steer even a requested topic around to something with which you feel comfortable.

Here are some of the things you ought to know about your audience. (You may not be able to get all this information, or you may get many other items, and some of the items listed are appropriate or useful in only certain cases.)

- The average age of the listeners, that is, young, middle-aged, elderly, or mixed. (If mixed, is there some way to get a profile?)
- The common interest(s) of the audience, as they relate to what you plan to present.
- Whether there is preponderance of males or females.

- Economic status of the members of the audience.
- Social or political interests.

IDENTIFYING YOUR GOAL

There are many possible goals in addressing an audience—to persuade, to enlighten, to amuse, to train, to educate, to indoctrinate, and perhaps still others. The point is that you must know what it is that you want your audience to *do* or *be* as a result of your speech, for example, believe, disbelieve, be better educated, be stimulated, be aroused, be amused. But make that a specific objective or set of objectives.

I want my proposal-writing students to understand the importance of successful proposal strategies and to know how to devise and develop them. The presenter at the Evelyn Wood free seminars on speed reading wants the listeners to sign up for the course. An Army recruiting sergeant making a speech to a high school graduating class wants the graduates to enlist in the Army.

DOING THE RESEARCH

How much research you need depends on not only how much you already know about the subject but on how up-to-date your knowledge is. Unless you are absolutely sure of what you know, it is good insurance to review the current literature on the subject. If you have a computer and modem or can gain access to such a system, you can turn also to the public databases for information and do a great deal of your research from your own office chair.

Initially, the research is aimed at guiding you in developing a good outline, identifying the key areas, as they relate to your main goal, and organizing the information in a logical order. There is more than one possible logical order, of course, depending on your purpose, so the logical order might be chronological, order of importance, deductive, inductive, or other. This is still an outlining/planning stage so you don't need to take voluminous notes yet. Still, it is a good idea to note any specific items that might be useful in the speech presentation, such as quotations, examples, definitions, metaphors, case histories, anecdotes, statistics, and other such items. (You might also note ideas for or availability of good visual aids at the appropriate points in the speech.)

It is never too early to note any items that appear to be good candidates for a brisk opening or smash finish. In fact, when researching materials for a speech or other presentation, even in the outline or early planning stage, I am alert for such items. If you consciously and deliberately seek such items at all times, you will soon condition your subconscious mind to do so, and you will almost automatically or instinctively recognize such items when you come across them.

A FEW PRACTICAL CONSIDERATIONS

One difficulty in preparing an outline is that it changes as you write it—as you research, think things out, and uncover new information, your outline needs almost constant revision. To overcome the physical problem of constant rewriting, some people use 3 × 5-inch index cards, which enable them to add information, shuffle and reorganize the cards, as necessary, and rewrite individual cards, instead of the entire outline. But today there is a far better way to do this: The "index cards" can be in your desktop computer, and be far easier to adjust, rewrite, shuffle, and reorganize. In fact, there are many computer programs designed especially to assist in the outlining process, and such programs can be used to produce "leaves" of textual data that can be transferred directly into first-draft manuscripts. In fact, the computer, with its word processor, outliner, and other programs that assist the writing process, has a great and salutary effect on writing. If at all possible, use a computer to do the work of writing your speeches.

Drafting, Revising, and Rewriting

There are two epigrams about writing and speechmaking that have been repeated so often they have become platitudes, if not absolute banalities. However, because they are in such popular use, I reluctantly repeat them here:

- *Tell them what you are going to tell them, tell them, then tell them what you told them.*

  This refers to the three parts of any presentation, the introduction, the body, and the conclusion. It states, simply, that you must introduce your subject, then present the content, and, finally, summarize what you presented. Of course it is greatly oversimplified. There is a bit more to organizing any presentation than this. We'll get to that in a moment.

- *KISS: Keep it simple, stupid.*

  Keeping a presentation "simple," in the sense of using straightforward sentences, familiar words, and direct style, is always good advice. (The word *stupid* is added strictly to create the acronym and it is entirely gratuitous.)

  I find it difficult to write in what some authorities deem to be "simple" writing. My mind simply does not work that way. I write long sentences and many complex sentences, with conjunctions, with dependent and independent clauses, and with much punctuation. I write slowly at times, feverishly at other times, with the result that many articles and other helper items are missing. I *re*write more simply. That is, in my many revisions I simplify. I break up many of those long, complex sentences and make them short, straightforward sentences. I install those missing articles. I eliminate unnecessary punctuation. I search out ambiguities and rephrase the statements. I do this over and over, and I hope, after many such revisions, that I have solved most of the problems. (I haven't. My editor will always find more, on almost every page.)

Self-editing, rewriting, and revision include doing all these things to simplify your language and correct errors, but it has an even more important function of sharpening the focus of your speech. Here is why: Unless you are an unusual writer, you almost surely over-write, including in your material a great deal more than the audience wants or needs to know about the subject. It is a common characteristic, and in most cases it is best to refrain from trying to combat it. Many writers, even the best of professional ones, find it a practical working habit to write and write, while the words flow easily, even though they know that much of what they are writing is excess baggage. It would be disastrous, usually, to shut off the flow of words; it is better to let it flow unchecked and edit the copy later. Hence, it is the rule, rather than the exception, to have gone into excessive detail. Editing consists in large part of trimming the copy by getting rid of the unnecessary detail. In fact, it has been observed by some professional editors that editing almost always means reducing the bulk of a manuscript by about one-third! (That is why one of the cliches of the writing profession is that all good writing is rewriting.)

That is one of the reasons that it is so important to have defined goals and objectives clearly. They are the standards against which you can later decide what material belongs in the manuscript and which should be excised from it. They permit you to keep a focus in mind as you edit and revise your copy.

What to Write First

With practice, each of us develops our own writing habits. Some writers take notes voluminously before even attempting an outline. Some begin with a rough outline that they revise steadily. Some begin with a lead, an introduction in which the writer does his thinking "on paper," writing and revising an approach to the subject. Some start in the middle of the subject, and some start at the beginning, as I do, knowing that they will revise the beginning as the last or penultimate act of writing. But despite the fact that we all develop certain writing habits of our own, there are logical arguments for certain approaches.

Designing an Opening

An argument is made by some for writing the close first, after first identifying objectives. In this scenario, the close must match your objectives, and the entire presentation is designed to culminate in that close. If you wish to follow this idea, make the search for a good close a priority in your initial research, immediately behind the definition of your primary objective, and develop the structure of your outline accordingly.

I am not in accord with this idea. I think it's more important to find ideas for a good opening to match the objectives, although the match may not be immediately apparent to the audience. I personally prefer an opening that telegraphs the central idea of the presentation, intimating to your audience where you are going, while stirring your audience immediately to full wakefulness.

Now this may appear to be in direct contradiction to the notion already stated that an introduction—the opening—is necessarily written last. If the introduction is written to match the body of the presentation, how can it be conceived in advance?

The answer is simple: The introduction is *rewritten* last. However, the basic premise upon which the presentation is based must be identified and articulated first. (At least, this is my own method for developing a presentation.) The idea is to offer an opening that is intriguing in some manner *and* establishes the theme.

Getting Ideas for Openings

One excellent method for achieving a brisk and attention-demanding opening is to open with something a bit startling, such as making a statement that appears to be an anomaly or paradox. Here are just a few examples:

- Exciting *insider* information, available to only the privileged
- Cryptic and mysterious information
- Short cuts and tips
- New ideas

For example, my usual opening in my proposal-writing seminar is the message that learning how to write winning proposals is not the true objective of the seminar, despite its billing as such: Learning how to win contracts is the true objective; proposals are only the means, not the end. (One of my most successful brochures announcing a proposal-writing seminar stated that the presentation was a "post-graduate course" in the art and was not for neophytes. Of course, that was an irresistible appeal to all, whether they were experienced proposal writers or beginners in the art.)

You should not make such startling statements casually. An opening statement such as this becomes the premise for the entire presentation, which must therefore be based on and prove the premise to be true. If you fail to furnish that proof, your presentation will be considerably less than a success. In my case, having made the statement, I must go on to focus my presentation on means and methods for winning contracts, although a chief tool for so doing is the proposal.

I have referred to and provided examples of how I introduce an all-day seminar. How would I adapt this idea to a speech of perhaps one hour or even a half-hour? Surely, there is a difference?

In fact, the difference is only one of degree, not of kind. A brief presentation, such as a speech, must be more specialized in the subject it addresses than an all-day seminar, of course, but it is still a presentation and still subject to the same basic rules and principles. I must choose some aspect of a subject that I can cover adequately in a shorter presentation—in a speech. Here is one way (in brief outline form) in which I might do so:

> TITLE OF SPEECH: *Proposal Cost Strategies*
> I: INTRODUCTION
>   You can appear to be the low bidder even when you are not.
> II: BODY OF PRESENTATION
>   How cost presentations must be made typically
>   How costs are evaluated
>   How to turn this to advantage to appear to be the low bidder
> III: Close
>   A significant quotation from a recognized authority or an illustrative anecdote with a surprise ending.

There are, of course, many other ways to find a premise such as this. Here are some alternative ideas:

- Three ways to organize and present a cost proposal
- How to develop a cost strategy
- Cost quotations make the difference.

Or suppose my general subject is proposal strategies. My opening and premise might be expressed in one of these ways:

- The four significant proposal strategies
- Devising and developing the capture strategy
- The customer dictates the strategy
- Winning through strategy.

The Dramatic Opening

Drama always inspires interest. Drama is conflict, with the resultant uncertainty of outcome. (Can you think of a successful novel, play, or movie that did not involve some kind of conflict?) If you can come up with a dramatic opening and follow it up suitably, you are quite likely to make a highly successful speech. Drama may have been implied in some of the foregoing ideas, but here are a few ideas for making the drama stark, as it should be to achieve your purpose:

- How to beat the competition
- You can fight City Hall and win
- Making your résumé the winner
- Overcoming the handicap of a speech impediment
- "Startling statistics" that make one sit up and pay attention.

Effective Closes

Closing, as used here, does not have the same meaning that it has when used by sales professionals. They use the term to mean asking the prospect for the order. The close we refer to here is the manner in which you conclude your speech effectively. Even an excellent speech is weakened by a close that is a whimper.

The close should be geared to and compatible with the overall theme, the objective, and the premise of the opening. There are many ways to close effectively. The thing to do is to leave the audience as alert and interested as they were when you uttered your opening, and to leave them with something to think about. Here are just a few of the many possibilities:

- The humorous close, using an anecdote that is pertinent to the message and objective of your speech, leaving your audience laughing
- The predictive close, a summary of what you have been presenting and a projection of what the future will bring vis-à-vis that discussion
- The authoritative quotation close, quoting what some highly respected person, contemporary or from the past, had to say on the subject
- The dramatic close, offering some "heavy" statement, perhaps citing some impressive statistics or highlight-

ing a battle yet to be waged and won, as relevant to your speech

- The novelty close, reporting some relevant but highly novel facts.

VISUAL AIDS

The right time to identify visual aids is while you are planning your speech, doing research and developing an outline. Mark the points in the outline where you see a need for some sort of visual aid.

There is more to the philosophy of how, where, and why to use visual aids than expediency. The first rule is to understand that the visual aid is as primary an instrument of communication as is the spoken or the written word. What this means is that you should be constantly weighing your words and the ideas you are trying to express to determine whether the words are adequate or if they are the most effective means for getting your message and meaning across to a listener. There is no doubt that words alone are a rather poor means for conveying many ideas and, especially, for conveying images. You might explain that some object is slightly oblate, but the average listener will not be enlightened because *oblate* is not that common a word. You could easily help the listener visualize this, however, with a simple drawing of an oblate object. Or you could use a verbal illustration by stating that the object is shaped like an orange, spherical, but flattened slightly at its poles. That will work because all of us know what an orange looks like. But try to explain a vector force with words alone to someone who has no idea what a vector is.

The consideration is not convenience or expediency but *need*. Do not use visual aids merely for a change of pace or to support language. Use visual aids where they are the best way to get your meaning across. But the inverse is also true. If a visual aid is not used to support text that is inadequate to the need, the visual aid should not require a great deal of words to support or explain it. That, in fact, is itself a measure of quality: A visual aid that requires a great deal of text to explain it is not doing much of a job and so it is not well conceived. When you conceive and develop visual aids, work at making them as self-sufficient as they possibly can be.

Creating Visual Aids

You do not have to rely on the services of an illustrator for the development of your visual aids. It is possible to create many of your own visual aids yourself with the equipment found in most offices today. Using a desktop computer, equipped with the proper software programs and a suitable printer, you can produce posters and charts of professional quality. You can use these as posters, handouts, or, using the office copier, you can make transparencies of these to use with an overhead projector.

OTHER PRESENTATION AIDS AND FEATURES

Unless you are the exception to the rule, you will want to spice your speech up with a few items to provoke a chuckle or two, if not a round of hearty guffaws. Finding such items should be a part of your research effort, but they need not be humorous anecdotes per se. There are many kinds of items that may or may not be humorous but are nevertheless useful to add credibility, spice, and general interest to your presentation. Here are some of those kinds of items:

- Quotations: Interesting, humorous, and/or thought-provoking statements from the speeches or writings of modern and contemporary individuals or from those of earlier times
- Anecdotes, humorous, dramatic, or otherwise interesting
- Models or samples
- Tables or matrices that are relevant.

SUMMARY

The key points made in this chapter may be used as a checklist in writing a speech:

[ ]   Am I clear on my general and specific subject?

[ ]   Have I defined my objective in precise terms?

[ ]   Have I done all my research?

[ ]   Am I the master of the subject now?

[ ]   Is my outline complete and up to date?

[ ]   Have I penciled in the visual and other aids I shall use?

[ ]   Do I have a provocative opening planned?

[ ]   Have I been over and over and over the draft until it shines?

[ ]   Is the premise of my opening clearly stated?

[ ]   Does my speech make good on supporting my premise?

[ ]   Will I leave them with something to think about?

11

Presenting the Presenter

The skills required to introduce speakers to the audience overlap with those required to be a good speaker, but there are a great many special considerations that the introducer ought to know.

THE GENTLE ART OF INTRODUCING OTHERS

Speakers are usually introduced to the audience by someone who acts as an introducer or master of ceremonies. But there is more involved in introductions than simply grinning at an audience and jubilantly announcing, "Here is Johnny Appleseed to tell us about apple trees."

Even in show business individual performers or guests are introduced properly, with a bit of ceremony and a bit of explanation. You can get as many samples of this as you wish by simply turning on your television. In the morning, you have a host of talk shows that feature guests. The strengths of the programs are only partly in the quality of the guests and the issues. The main attractions and strengths of these programs are the hosts. In the Johnny Carson show, Carson is introduced by Ed McMahon, and he, in turn, is both performer and host who does the remaining introductions himself. Certainly it is he who is responsible for the show's popularity. On some weekend days—Sundays, especially—you have prominent newsmen and women hosting and leading discussion groups composed of other newspeople and assorted notables whose knowledge or opinion is of interest at the moment. But no matter how well known those guests are—Henry Kissinger or Gerald Ford, for example—each gets properly introduced to the audience.

The introducer who presents speakers at business and community functions must play a slightly different role, in that the introducer must be somewhat self-effacing. The introducer must not step on the speaker's lines or otherwise dim the spotlight that should shine on the featured speaker. Your role as an introducer is to smooth the way for your speaker and help him or her to be as successful as possible on the dais.

Introducing others is itself a presentation or perhaps a series of presentations. Don't sell it short; it can be a most important element of the program and calls for good presentation skills as well. Moreover, it is not an unworthy role or an unimportant part of the program. As they say in the theater, there are no small parts, but only small actors and actresses.

In some programs, the host introduces only the first speaker, and if there are other speakers to follow, each speaker introduces the next speaker. That is, however, more the exception than the rule; it is usually practiced in only quite informal circumstances. The more usual practice is to have a host introduce each speaker and make all special announcements. When the first speaker has finished, for example, the host waits for the applause to subside and then mounts the rostrum with a, "Thank you, Charlie. That was quite wonderful. And now let's welcome the distinguished Mister Jonathan So–and–so, who will talk to us today about noise pollution in New York City. Mr. So–and–so has an impressive array of credentials. . . ."

Now that appears to be the easiest kind of platform job to handle, does it not? But it has its mishaps and assorted hazards too, just as making the main speech does. Murphy's law is hard at work here too, trying earnestly to see to it that anything that can go wrong will do so.

WHAT DOES A GOOD INTRODUCTION INCLUDE?

There are more than a few jests to the effect that the best speech is one in which the conclusion is close to the introduction. True or not, it is fair to say that the introduction of a speaker ought to be brief—not more than a few minutes—but it ought also to be complete, if it is to achieve its purpose, which, stated as briefly as possible, is to do the following:

- Make the speaker's name clear.
- Explain who the speaker is.
- Explain what he or she will talk about.

These are two separate and distinct problems that arise all too often in situations where you must introduce a speaker, especially a speaker on whom you have never laid eyes before. You leap confidently to the platform to announce to all that today it is their great fortune to listen to none other than the celebrated Clair de Lune herself, but up steps Henrietta Bouffant. And you don't know the difference, never having laid eyes on either one.

You have failed to get the word that Clair de Lune was taken ill suddenly and Henrietta Bouffant is a last-minute substitute. It is an embarrassing situation for both of you, although Madam Bouffant may be experienced enough and tranquil enough to pass it off with some light remark, such as, "Well thank you very much, Jo. That's the third time this week I have been mistaken for that gorgeous Clair de Lune."

But even when you get the name right, you must get the pronunciation right. It is easy enough to make the name "George Jones" clear. Everyone who is literate knows how to spell "George" and "Jones" and recognizes the names readily enough. But you don't get many guest speakers with names that easy. If you were introducing Nobel Prize winner

Subrahmanyan Chancrasekhar to an audience, you might have some difficulty even pronouncing the name, let alone briefing the audience on how to pronounce it themselves. So one thing you must do is be sure that you know the speaker's name, how it is pronounced, and how it is spelled. If it is a difficult one, you should practice saying it a few times until you have it exactly right.

Even for less difficult names, there is often a problem. How do you pronounce "McLeod?" Is it "Mac-lee-odd," "Mic-klowd," or something else? And suppose the printed information you have says that your speaker is "Barbra Britton." Is that truly pronounced "Barb-rah" or is it a typo and actually pronounced "Bar-bah-rah?"

There are many whose names are of foreign origin, retaining the original spelling. Whether they have Anglicized the pronunciation or retained the Old World pronunciation is often not clear. How does Robert Guillaume prefer his name be pronounced? or Robert Goulet?

Most of us are rather sensitive about our names, although those with unusual or different names tend to get inured to hearing the pronunciation of their names mangled and may even be amused by it—but not on formal occasions, such as when they are to deliver an address. What may be amusing when committed by a store clerk or delivery man becomes a serious offense when committed by a host, who had the time, the means, and the obligation to get it right.

The best way to minimize the possibility of such an error is to verify all your information shortly before you mount the platform. Check and make sure the guest you have listed is at hand and ready. If there is more than one speaker, check on the others as well, preferably individually and separately, just before you must do the introduction. Try to meet with the speaker personally to verify your facts and your pronunciation of the name. Normally, the speaker should have provided information for the introduction, but it is still a good idea to go over the information with the speaker and verify it.

When you do the introduction, do not appear to be reading it mechanically, even if you are reading a portion of it. You may glance at the notes you have, but make your presentation with your eyes on the audience, meeting the eyes of several people seated before you. Mention the speaker's name several times and stress his or her credentials. Make the audience feel privileged to be able to hear the words of this gifted individual, as you make this speaker aware that you fully appreciate and are impressed by his or her credentials and are a sincere booster.

Explain Who the Speaker Is

Perhaps you would not have had to explain who Albert Einstein was, had it fallen to you to introduce him to an audience, but there are few individuals, no matter how accomplished, as well-known as Einstein was. I am no luminary, so my introducer has a job before him or her to justify my appearance on the platform and explain my qualifications for taking up the audience's valuable time. But that is the usual case.

Usually, the information you use here, biographical data, comes from the speaker. Unfortunately, few of us are able to ever see ourselves as others see us or even as a completely objective, rational analysis would portray us. Thus, the biographical notes a speaker offers as a suggested introduction may be grossly inflated and egocentric, or it may be overly modest, revealing far too little and taking far too little credit for oneself. (The latter is not at all unusual; many highly accomplished individuals do not take themselves very seriously and are not at all impressed with themselves.)

Your job as introducer is to find the truth between these extremes, and you must usually dig to find it if you happen not to know much about the individual. One way to do this is to track down and array the simple facts about the individual, to wit:

- Education: where, when, what subjects, what degrees
- Present and past positions
- Memberships and posts held

- Publications
- Patents
- Honors and awards
- Listings (e.g., Who's Who)
- Citations in other publications and/or articles written about.

It is not difficult to collect this information. In fact, the most practical thing to do is to make up a simple questionnaire form listing these, plus a large section for remarks and notes, and ask the speaker to fill it out. You won't need any more than this, in most cases.

However, you may and should, if possible, gather up far more details than you have time or need to present. You must then edit the material down to manageable size, perhaps two or three minutes' worth. The standard for doing so is simple enough: Your purpose in explaining who the speaker is goes beyond mere introduction for its own sake. It has the more serious purpose of presenting the speaker's credentials to speak on the subject on which he or she will speak. Use that objective of establishing proper credentials—not credentials generally, but credentials to speak on the specific subject chosen—as a screen for determining what materials stay and which are discarded.

By all means, eliminate all tedious and irrelevant detail. It is rarely of interest to learn about the speaker's family, church, many memberships that are unrelated to his subject and his reason for standing before this audience. Cull out all questionable items and use the most pertinent and most interesting ones only.

Explain What the Speaker Will Talk About

The title of a presentation may—but often does not—furnish a substantial clue to the nature of the presentation, what it will be about in general terms. Even when it does that is not enough. In explaining what the subject is, you should announce a few highlights of such a nature as to furnish the attendees a reason to be there and to be interested. Whether you announce the formal title or not (and it is not absolutely necessary to do so), do explain a little of what the presentation is to be. List a few of the most outstanding features and try to do so in terms of how the listener will benefit. Where do you get this information? From the speaker, of course.

For example, if I am giving a presentation on how to launch an independent consulting practice, I will tell my introducer that among the topics I will discuss and provide answers for are these: Should one incorporate? What are the alternative ways of organizing a professional practice? How does one get started winning the first few clients? Does one need a lawyer, an accountant, or other help to incorporate? What are the chief hazards?

A good introducer ought to ask the speaker for a summary of the presentation he will make, preferably as a list of key points expressed in simple language. Explain why you wish these and ask the speaker to list the items he or she thinks are most important.

Announcing such items as these alerts the audience immediately and helps ensure their close attention for they almost surely want the answers to these and many other questions. Of course, the speaker may present these promises him- or herself, but it is usually far more effective to have the introducer do so in advance. It creates anticipation and suspense, two excellent emotions supporting a speaker.

It is perfectly okay to have the information written out, either as a text (script) or as a set of notes, and to refer to this. However, do not read a script to the audience. Study the material until you know it, and deliver it as thought it were completely spontaneous.

A FEW DO'S AND DON'TS

You may shine briefly on the platform by striking a light note and even telling a humorous anecdote. In fact, some speakers prefer to have the introducer break the ice by evoking a first laugh from the audience. They find that it makes their job much easier. But don't overdo this. The speaker is the star of the evening and stars do not need to reflect light from elsewhere.

Don't get too flowery in your introduction. Avoid the superlatives and the hyperbole in general. Even a speaker with a slightly swollen ego can be embarrassed by this or may even feel that you are leading the audience to expect too much and make it difficult for him or her to live up to your hype.

Avoid the tired old cliches and platitudes. Here are a few examples:

Our speaker needs no introduction. (So why are you introducing him?)

Heeeressss _____. (Leave that line to Ed McMahon.)

Without further ado. . . . (That line would make anyone cringe.)

It is indeed a privilege and an honor. . . . (That one has whiskers too.)

If you must err, it is better to err on the side of saying too little, rather than too much, and being too simple rather than too ornate with your language. State what you have to state, tell your little anecdote (if you have one to tell) facing your audience. Then give your speaker his cue to step forward or ascend the dais, as the case may be, by saying to your audience something along the lines of, "Ladies and gentlemen, I give you Ed Wilson—" and, turning to Wilson—"Ed?" As he comes forward you lead the applause, and when he arrives where you are standing you extend your hand for a hearty handshake and depart. Your role is completed until Wilson has finished or until there is a break where you have some announcement to make.

12

Preparing for the Impromptu Speech

Professionals are always prepared to
be unprepared to speak.

WHEN BRAVE FOLKS QUAKE

Even the most experienced speakers quake at being called
upon to "say a few words" when they are totally unprepared
to speak. But then the most experienced speakers are only
rarely totally unprepared. They anticipate the possibility that
they will be called on and have at least mentally framed a few
thoughts, if not actually rehearsed a brief presentation. That
is most often the reason that some individuals can stand up
when called upon and deliver an apparently spontaneous
speech that sparkles as it moves smoothly and surely along to
make its points and end memorably.

Even in a conference room, with a handful of others
seated about a long table, you might be suddenly and unexpectedly asked for your opinion or reaction to some matter
under discussion. Do you stammer that you have not had
time yet to think about it or beg off even expressing an opinion? Probably not. It is most difficult to dodge a request to

speak when asked to, whether the occasion is a meeting, a large banquet, a small dinner party, a conference, or any other event.

Once you have been a speaker anywhere at any time, and anyone in the room knows that you have delivered at least one speech without rendering everyone within earshot unconscious, there is an excellent possibility that you will be called upon. However, for occasions on which you think there is a serious possibility that someone will call on you for a few words, it is not necessary to have a lengthy, formal address prepared. "A few words" ought to be just that, a few words. They should, on most occasions, not be more than five or ten minutes of words, at most. However, as Woodrow Wilson and others have observed, it is far easier to make a two-hour speech without preparation than a five- or ten-minute one; the brief speech needs ample preparation, time to gather the words and boil them down to that precious few. And so, if you are to speak well and yet be brief, you need to prepare a few notes, documenting basic data about the occasion and listing cues for yourself to guide you in choosing wisely the few words you will use. These are the kinds of questions to which you need answers:

- What is the occasion? (Awards dinner? Victory party? Annual meeting? Formal luncheon? Meeting with and presentation to a prospective client? Contract negotiation? Professional symposium?)
- Who will be there? (Individual names and/or functional titles and identities of probable attendees.)
- What are the most probable subjects of discussion?
- Who are likely to be the scheduled speakers?
- Who else is likely to be asked to "rise to the occasion?"
- What are they likely to say?
- What kinds of questions will most likely be raised?
- Are there to be attendees of known biases or positions?
- What, if any, are the most controversial issues?

- How do others probably conceive of your role and/or position?
- What questions are you most likely to be asked?
- On what subjects might your opinions be solicited?

Once you have asked and answered these questions, you are ready to do some informal planning. If necessary, gather a few statistics or other facts and figures, and make suitable notes on cue cards. Prepare a general outline, key words to remind you of the thoughts you had. (Index cards (3 × 5 inch) work well for this kind of note.)

You may prepare notes or key words for an hour's talk, although you should not expect to speak for more than a few minutes. That's one advantage of using the index cards: You use them selectively to deliver a few minutes of words on whatever appears to be most appropriate. In fact, while you are in attendance and others are speaking, you may do some planning mentally to select the ones you will want, as you begin to perceive what will be most appropriate for you to say.

THE *MOST* IMPORTANT WORDS

As in making any speech, and perhaps even more so for the brief impromptu address, the opening and closing words are probably more important than the words that come between them. Avoid that completely trite and banal "Unaccustomed as I am to public speaking" and any derivative sentence bearing any resemblance to it. No alibis or apologies are needed, appropriate, or helpful. No one cares or will think about whether you are or are not accustomed to public speaking unless you raise the subject yourself. Also, avoid explaining that you were not expecting to be called upon and have not prepared anything. Just launch into your address in an informal, conversational tone.

The same philosophy applies to your closing. Make no explanations that you have done the best you could under the circumstances or otherwise appear to be apologizing for not being William Jennings Bryan or some other silver-tongued orator. However, both openings and closings ought to be bright and snappy. There are several ways and things you can do to achieve this effect:

- Appropriate humor is always a good device for both openings and closings. Just be sure that the humor is completely relevant to your remarks.

- Preferably, open with an anecdote that illustrates and introduces your main thought, and close with one that sums it up. The anecdote need not be humorous. It is much more important that it be relevant, as an introduction to, illustration of, or summation of your main point.

- Humanize the anecdote and give it immediacy by relating it as something within your own experience or that of someone you know. Use names, even if they are fictitious ones, and relate it as a most recent experience, if possible. These are the elements that breathe life into the anecdote.

- If you cannot find suitable anecdotes, quotations, especially by well-known persons, living or dead, will often serve the purpose almost equally well. "Mark Twain once said, 'It usually takes me more than three weeks to prepare a good impromptu speech'" is not a bad way to introduce a brief lecture on that subject, is it? One might even use that to close a few words on the subject, adding some remark to signify thorough agreement with Twain.

13

Panels, Moderators, and Leaders

A committee has been described as a group of people who singly can do nothing, but who together decide that nothing can be done; a discussion panel is usually a bit more productive than that, since they usually operate before an audience who listen, observe, and ask questions.

A BRIEF SUMMARY OF PANEL ARRANGEMENTS AND PROCEDURES

Once you enter the world of public speaking and presentations you are quite likely to be asked to appear on a panel or as part of a discussion group, and possibly even to be a panel leader and moderator. This is not a fearful prospect. There are many considerations to commend the panel approach. Perhaps the greatest comfort, from your viewpoint as a panel member, is that there is a much lower level of anxiety for you in making presentations in this manner as compared with standing alone on the dais. You share any stress equally with your fellow panelists! And if there is any blame or censure for anything going wrong, you may be equally generous in sharing it with the others.

A panel may vary in number, although the range is most often from a low of three to a high of eight or ten. A panel is most often gathered to discuss and present an agreed-upon subject before an audience, frequently accepting questions or even comments and challenges from the audience, and perhaps permitting some of the discussions to settle into mini-debates. One member of the panel is the leader or moderator, controlling the discussions and questions from the audience and managing the program overall. That is a most important job, requiring leadership, management, mediation, and diplomacy.

Typically, the panel is seated behind a table on a platform, facing the audience. The moderator is generally seated in the center, although in some cases the moderator stands to one side with a ready microphone.

The moderator acts as the host, introducing him- or herself to the audience, presenting the subject and agenda to the audience and to the panel, and explaining how the discussion will be conducted. He or she then introduces each panel member by name and title, with an introduction including the panelist's background, special achievements, or other relevant matters of note.

A typical agenda for a panel is to allot each member a segment of time to make a presentation—15 to 30 minutes—and then taking questions from the audience. The moderator is in control. He or she will gracefully cut off a panelist who is running beyond the time allocation and will control the flow of questions, selecting the individuals from whom questions are accepted, trying to ensure that questions are accepted from all segments of the audience and that everyone in the audience has an equal chance to be heard. A question from the audience may be directed by the questioner to an individual panelist or to the panel generally. In the latter case, the moderator may redirect the question to one panelist or may invite the panelists to volunteer to answer. Often, even if a panelist has given a complete answer, the moderator will invite other panelists to make any comments they think appropriate.

If you are to be a panelist you should prepare a brief presentation, which you may deliver seated or standing (usually) as you wish. You can then expect to participate in answering questions and in follow-up discussions, as necessary. If you are the moderator, you have more complex duties and responsibilities.

GUIDELINES FOR A PANELIST

Bear in mind first and foremost that as a panelist you are only one part of the program, probably less than 20 percent. Unlike the situation where you star as the main speaker, as a panelist you occupy the spotlight only briefly and intermittently. Do not try to dominate question-answering or any follow-up discussions with a spectator. Above all, be discreet when you disagree with your fellow panelists, with someone in the audience, or with your moderator. Avoid scrupulously all dogmatic statements and shows of impatience, even if you are convinced that you are arguing with a boob. Once in a while you will encounter a quarrelsome know-it-all panel- or audience-member. Nothing is to be gained by putting such a person down except to destroy the work of the panel.

If you have been invited to handle a topic in which you think yourself to be unqualified, don't accept the assignment. Such mistakes happen occasionally, and the best thing to do is to explain honestly that you would be out of your depth in that subject and would not serve the panel well.

When you do answer a question, do not deliver a lecture on the subject; You do not have to tell the audience everything you know about it. Stick strictly to the question and deliver a direct answer, being as brief as possible, consistent with providing a proper answer. Remember that there are several others on the panel, and they may wish to have a minute or two to offer their own views. Performing on a panel is not a soloist's role.

This does not mean that you may not use a bit of well-placed humor or a cogent quotation or epigram. Each time you speak, you are making at least a mini-presentation, and all the guidelines cited earlier in these pages are valid here, modified only as necessary to meet the guidelines of this chapter.

One problem you may encounter is that of having an inexperienced moderator or one who is not firm enough in handling some of the problems. For that reason alone, it is advisable that you have a good grasp of all the things that a good moderator ought to do to exercise and maintain control. For example, suppose the panelist who precedes you runs over his or her allotted time and refuses to end the presentation despite signals from the moderator to do so. You may help the moderator by breaking in with something such as, "Thank you. That was a great explanation." And then you press on with your own presentation. Even a stubborn panelist will usually hesitate to oppose both the moderator and another panelist whose time he or she is treading on.

YOUR CHORES AS MODERATOR

When you are the moderator of a panel discussion, your duties and responsibilities are both technical and managerial. Although you have introduced each panelist to the audience, it is a good plan to place a prominent nameplate before each member of the panel. The panelist's name ought to be in the largest letters possible for maximum legibility, and lettered on both sides of the name plate so that the panelists, as well as the audience, can each read the nameplates. (Most often, the panelists will not know each other prior to the meeting.)

As the moderator you will have to know the agenda thoroughly (or perhaps you have even prepared it yourself). You must have a good grasp of the topic and know what each panelist will have to say about it. Your role in controlling every element of the program is important. There are a number of important factors in a panel program, but these are the three main elements:

1. The initial presentations by the panelists
2. Accepting questions from the audience
3. The responses to the questions by the panelists.

As noted, you must be sure that each panelist does not exceed his or her allotted time for his or her initial presentation. You will have a schedule, as well as an agenda, and you must allow for the time planned for questions from the audience and responses to those questions. In many cases that is the main purpose of the panel discussion. (If the purpose was discussion among experts for other use than presentation to the public, you would probably have formed a study group, rather than a panel.)

Logically, the flow and objectives are as depicted in Figure 8. It is your duty as moderator to encourage this flow and see to it that it takes place as it should.

As moderator you must observe the audience closely, giving everyone a fair chance to ask questions and be heard if they have comments or challenges. Typically, you will find a few individuals who would dominate the audience participation if permitted to. You must guard against this and be sure that others have their opportunity.

It is usually a good idea to repeat the question asked from the audience in a loud, clear voice so that everyone can hear it. You may even have to rephrase the question yourself to make it clear.

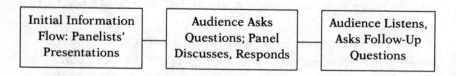

Initial Information Flow: Panelists' Presentations	Audience Asks Questions; Panel Discusses, Responds	Audience Listens, Asks Follow-Up Questions

Figure 8 Basic information flow from panel to audience.

Typical Problems in Moderating a Panel

You do need to be pleasant and smooth, but you may run into occasions when you must get quite firm. Here are a few typical problems and suggested solutions:

- Some panelists run over their allotted time for their initial presentation and stubbornly ignore the moderator's signal to end their presentation. As a moderator, you may be forced to smile and say, when you encounter this, "I'm sorry Mr. Smith, but your time is up," and turn immediately to the next panelist with a cue to begin the next presentation.

- The same thing applies to the answering of questions. Although the panelists ought to know better, occasionally one will not be content with a simple answer to a question, but will attempt to deliver a lengthy lecture on the subject. Again, as moderator, you must break in firmly and end the lecture.

- You may encounter similar problems with persistent members of the audience who try to dominate the question and answer sessions and shout down others. Again, this requires maintaining a strong hand. You must be in charge and in control.

14

Seminar Presentations

Seminars are increasingly popular as both a marketing tool and an income-producing source of activity in itself.

A DEFINITION

A seminar was originally an academic term for a group of advanced university students engaged in a special study. The term has become broadened over the years. Today's seminar is an instructional session which addresses a specialized subject and ranges from an hour or two to several days. It may be led by a single instructor or by a staff of instructors. It may consist entirely of lectures, or include demonstrations and exercises, or include a great deal of open discussion. It may include breaking down into a number of small groups for smaller group instruction or exercises as part of the format.

J. Stephen Lanning, Executive Director, Consultants National Resource Center and publisher of *Consulting Opportunities Journal*, said "A great many of my subscribers and clients take advantage of the opportunities offered them by seminars and workshops. Seminars are a key marketing tool, as well as a source of income, for many professionals. In fact, one subscriber has reduced the process to a formula. He uses three speaking tools: One—The one-hour luncheon talk. He uses this as a marketing tool for his full-day seminar, which he outlines in this talk. Two—The two-to-four-hour workshop. Here, this consultant develops one or two topics at some length. He uses this tool at national conventions and conferences, customizing it in each case. And three—The full-day seminar."

Seminars are used by businesses and other organizations in at least two ways: First, as training presentations for learning purposes, with the overall objective of direct income, since these seminars involve registration and attendance fees; and second, as sales presentations for marketing purposes, with the overall objective of sales.

Seminars, even those offered as pure sales presentations, are presented as learning sessions, each focused on a single subject, such as negotiation with labor unions, contract law, copy writing, speed reading, or other practical topics. In most cases the approach is "how–to"—how to write a contract, how to use a computer, how to negotiate with labor, how to develop software, or how to market services. But within that general framework many variations are possible, and you must think out your design carefully.

The distinguishing features are simply a specialized subject and a relatively short duration, rarely more than a week and most commonly one or two days, although there are seminars of less than a full day also.

Seminars can be and are used as effective marketing promotions. Many organizations offer free seminars for that purpose. The Evelyn Wood speed reading school advertised weekly free seminars in this area for a number of years. Albert Lowry, the butcher turned real estate tycoon, used many free seminars to promote his $500 weekend paid seminar in how to make money in real estate.

Presenters opt far more often for "pure" seminars than for workshops, and workshops are rarely "pure" workshops, but are sessions that are part seminar and part workshop.

However, few issues in this world are black and white, and seminars are no exception. Even those seminars that make no claim to being workshops are often designed to include at least some degree of direct participation by attendees, such as open discussion, individual responses to questions posed by the presenter, brainstorming, or group participation of another sort. So whether a session should be referred to as a seminar or workshop depends on what the *principal* activity is, although there is a distinct tendency to refer to all such sessions as seminars, regardless of the format and nature of the content.

SEMINARS ARE USUALLY "HOW TO" PRESENTATIONS

The almost universal tendency to designate every session a seminar, rather than a workshop, may appear a bit anomalous, because the most dominant emphasis in seminars is on the "how to" approach. That is apparent in seminar literature, even in the titles, such as the following titles listed in a recent seminar brochure announcement that crossed my own desk:

- How to Be an Assertive Manager
- How to Buy Printing and Related Services
- Training and Computers Seminar: How to Teach People to Use Computers
- How to Work with Customers
- Proposals and Competition: How to Develop Winning Proposals
- How to Supervise People
- How to Get Things Done
- How to Write and Design Sales Literature

Even when the words "how to" are not used in the title, the how-to nature of the coverage is clearly implied:

- Developing Applications with dBase III Plus
- Networking IBM Personal Computers
- Writing Effective Advertising
- Designing and Preparing Camera-Ready Artwork
- Basic Supervision Seminar
- Advance Supervision Skills
- Strategic Planning for Database
- Logical and Physical Design for Relational Database Management Systems
- Analyzing and Improving Direct Mail
- Desktop Publishing: A Practical Tutorial Featuring Product Comparisons
- PC LANs: Hardware, Software, and Applications
- X.25: Evaluating and Selecting Offerings and Options
- The IBM PC XT/AT and Compatibles: Maximizing Their Potential
- Performance Measurement Systems and C/S Data Usage
- Power Communication Skills for Women

To confirm the how-to philosophy of the design, the descriptions of the seminar content—and every one of the 23 programs listed is described and referred to as a seminar—contain many more how-to lists, such as these lines taken at random from many of the 23 program descriptions:

- How to Test Your Own Assertiveness
- How to Settle Disputes
- How to Configure Your Machine
- How to Evaluate Vendors' Products
- How to Delegate for Success
- How to Overcome Obstacles
- How to Assure That the Design Supports the Message
- How to Avoid Major Copywriting Errors

- How to Make the Right Decisions
- How to Get the Facts
- How to Use Photos and Illustrations to Sell
- How to Deal with Sabotage
- How to Deal with People Who Intimidate
- How to Deflect Unfair Criticism

WHY THE "HOW TO" ORIENTATION

There is emphasis on the how-to in seminar programs simply because that is why most people come to seminars—to acquire specific skills. Most adults do not return to the learning process to further their general education; most believe that they have had enough of that. Seminar attendees want to learn how to win contracts, how to win promotions, how to use a computer, how to survive office politics, etc. Employers are also motivated to train people to be more effective. They spend thousands of dollars to train people to become better managers, write more winning proposals, manage payables and receivables more efficiently, and otherwise contribute more to company success. The goal that attracts attendees and motivates employers to pay for employees to attend seminars is not learning per se but some specific, promised benefit that appears to be a likely result.

It should thus be clear that in planning a seminar the following aims ought to be kept clearly in mind:

1. Have as a specific goal a direct, practical benefit for the attendee and/or the employer who pays for the attendance.
2. Be a definite "how to" session to impart practical skills.
3. Include materials as presentation aids, learning aids, demonstrations, and handouts.
4. Include exercises and practice sessions, if and as necessary.

5. Provide ample opportunity for attendees to ask questions and participate in open discussions.
6. Identify the credentials of presenters and materials promised.

HANDOUTS

Attendees at seminars, especially those of full-day or longer duration, have both a practical and a psychological need to carry away from the seminar something more than notes scribbled on a pad or in a notebook. Many seminar presenters offer each attendee a folder with a number of brochures and handout sheets, but by far the most popular and useful handout is a full seminar manual which gives the attendee a full printed version of the substance of the seminar. That may be a book or manual published commercially, or it may be a seminar manual made up especially for the occasion. An outline, that is, the table of contents of such a manual (on proposal writing, in this case) is shown in Figure 9 on page 174.

Figure 10 illustrates the table of contents of a seminar manual is another exhibit, one showing a typical page of the manual. Please note in that latter exhibit that the text of the page is arranged to leave about one-third of the page blank, with the heading "NOTES," inviting the attendee to use the blank space for this purpose. This is not only a great convenience for the attendees but serves the greater purpose of permitting them to make the notes in the most useful places. I also print the manual on one side only so that the reverse side is blank. That is, whenever the attendee is looking at any page of the text, the left hand page is blank and may also be used to make notes opposite the appropriate text passages of the manual.

MAKING THE PRESENTATION

You have a number of options in making the presentation, which include doing it yourself, wholly or in part, and getting

TABLE OF CONTENTS

Figure 9 Contents of seminar manual.

VIII: THE ART OF WRITING WELL

*A few miscellaneous and useful ideas
acquired over the years.*

WHAT DOES "WRITING WELL" MEAN?

Writing well, contrary to what appears to be the conviction of many who profess to teach the art of writing, is not really a matter of grammar and punctuation nearly so much as it is a matter of information and organization. Weaknesses in the mechanics of using the language are easily shored up by the editing processes. Weaknesses in information and presentation are fatal, beyond the healing powers of even the most capable editing.

TIPS ON WRITING WELL

Some of the most valuable tips on writing well have been given already: stick to nouns and verbs, and minimize the use of adjectives and adverbs; shun hyperbole; quantify as much as possible and do not round off numbers; and be specific, rather than general, by making positive statements and offering as much detail as possible. But the real principle underlying much of this advice has been presented, but not yet linked up with the act of writing well. It is this: The ability to provide specific information, details, and quantified information is excellent evidence that you know what you are talking about, just as the inability—or, at least, the failure—to do so suggests that you do not know what you are talking about, but are only being glib—trying to "wing it," in the hope of muddling through somehow.

AN OPERATING PRINCIPLE

That same principle applies to writing itself: by far the most common cause of bad writing is not the inability of the writer to find the right words and/or organize the information.

Figure 10 Typical page of manual with space for notes.

others to do so or help to do so, along the lines of various patterns, from hiring a presenter to inviting other consultants to be guest speakers and taking advantage of services offered by many organizations, as discussed earlier. Of all the options, however, none offers the same benefits and advantages that doing it yourself does.

Why You Should Do It Yourself

The benefits of producing seminars are far greater when you make the presentation yourself, rather than through the words and mouths of others. Aside from the obvious benefit of minimizing costs and gaining prestige, there is the increasing skill in making presentations generally. A full-day seminar affords you far greater opportunity to improve your skills and develop a platform personality than does the shorter lecture presentation.

CLASSROOM OR THEATER STYLE?

When you arrange to rent a meeting room at some hotel in which to conduct your seminar, you will usually be asked whether you want to have the seating arranged in classroom or theater style. (If the hotel manager neglects to ask you, you must remember to raise the subject yourself or you will probably find your meeting room arranged theater style, which may not be what you want.) Theater style is, as the term suggests, simple rows of chairs, as in a theater. Classroom style, however, places attendees at tables.

Theater style is fine, generally, for brief presentations, even seminars, if they last only an hour or two. However, if you are presenting a seminar that goes on all day or even more than one day, theater style can get pretty uncomfortable after an hour or two. Moreover, if attendees have brought briefcases and notebooks, and if you have given them a package of handouts to which they will want to make references, theater style seating is truly inadequate. And, finally, it is rather awkward to make notes seated in an audience arranged in theater style. Your attendees will not like the arrangement very well after a few hours.

EVALUATIONS BY ATTENDEES

It is more or less customary to solicit from seminar attendees their opinions of the seminar in enough detail to diagnose and, if possible, improve future presentations of the seminar. The mechanism and a few guidelines for doing so will be covered in Chapter 15.

15

Useful Additional Information

Making successful presentations in the business world involves much more than merely speaking in public; following are some related concerns that may affect you as a manager or as a speaker—or perhaps as both.

EVALUATIONS AND CRITIQUES

It is a fairly common practice today to ask audiences to evaluate and critique formal presentations, especially seminar programs. Typically, the sponsor of the program hands out a form (it is often simply included in the initial handout packet) and asks attendees to fill it out before leaving. The form includes a place for signing it, but usually the readers are advised that identifying themselves on the evaluation form is entirely voluntary, and that it is perfectly acceptable to submit the form unsigned if they wish. It is far more important at this point to get an objective reaction than to get a quotable comment.

The form has as its main overall purpose the improvement of the program. The sponsor wishes to have several areas evaluated:

- The speaker(s)
- The handout materials
- The content
- The length
- The cost

In addition to specific critiques of these matters, the sponsor is interested in any suggestions attendees may have for improving the program and/or for presenting other, additional programs.

As a presenter, such evaluations should be of great personal concern to you, for they are far better mirrors than any other you can find. They enable you to see yourself as others see you. To the extent that attendees are willing to be entirely frank, and to the extent that their judgments are typical and reflect consensus, you can use this information to improve your presentations.

Designing the Form

Designing an evaluation form is much like designing a questionnaire in the basic principles and guidelines. Bear in mind that you are really asking for *opinions,* and the opinions are those of lay persons, not experts. In fact, you don't want the opinions of experts. You don't want clinical opinions at all. You want the reactions of those who are typical attendees. You want to know what the perceptions of your audiences are. Those are the opinions that count.

With that in mind, here are some basic ideas and guidelines in designing an evaluation form, as compared to the design of questionnaires:

1. Only a relatively small percentage of people asked to fill out questionnaires do so. One reason few do so is that most questionnaires are tedious and tiresome in one or both of two characteristics: They are far too long and far too difficult to complete, requiring too

much mental effort. Everyone has an opinion on most subjects, and most people are eager enough to be critics on most subjects, but they are usually unwilling to go to great trouble to indulge such tendencies. Therefore, to the extent that you can make the instrument easy to respond to, you can improve the response.

Most attendees will accommodate your wishes and fill out an evaluation form for you. However, if it is too long, some attendees won't be bothered with it or they won't fill it out entirely, but will make only a general response that will not be especially helpful. Keep the evaluation form to one page, and that not too densely populated with items calling for responses.

2. You are trying to determine the average or typical opinion. There will always be a few extreme opinions, ranging from those people who absolutely thoroughly appreciated every aspect of the session to those people who positively abhorred everything they saw and heard. Don't be unduly influenced by the extremes. They are usually (but not always) the exceptions and not the typical reactions.

3. Establish specific points to be checked and use a simple scale—poor, fair, good, excellent. Don't ask attendees to rate "on a scale of 1 to 10" or to indicate on a graphic representation of a scale, such as "1.....5.....10.....15.....20." When asked to judge according to such a method, there is a great tendency to rate most items in the middle, and that is not at all helpful to an overall evaluation.

4. Don't ask for an essay for each item. Many people hate to write or think; both represent hard work and are energetically resisted. Make the items check-offs as much as possible, requiring some thought and judgment but not such shallow cerebrations as "go/no-go," "true-false" or "good-bad." Give them a bit more range of choice than that. But don't go to the opposite extreme and provide too many alternatives; for example,

outstanding, excellent, very good, good, fair, poor, very poor are too many choices to choose among.

5. Do provide space and an invitation to write any comments, suggestions, or critiques they wish to volunteer, but don't bank on getting too many responses to this invitation.

6. Do ask attendees to respond to each of the critical items listed, except for cost. If you pose that question directly, almost all will tell you the cost was too high! You'll find out about the attendees' reactions to cost indirectly through their responses to general questions, such as "What did you like best? What least?" and "Would you recommend this seminar to others?"

Our sample evaluation form offers a general idea of how such a form may be organized and what it might cover. Feel free to adapt the form to your specific situation. If, for example, you have several speakers, you will have to expand that area and provide space to rate each speaker individually and, possibly, comparatively.

EVALUATION

1. Coverage was   Too detailed [ ]   Not detailed enough [ ]
   Just right [ ]
   Comment: _____

2. Seminar was   Too long [ ]   Not long enough [ ]   Just about
   right [ ]
   Comment: _____

3. Speaker was   Poor [ ]   Fair [ ]   Good [ ]   Excellent [ ]
   because: _____
   Comment: _____

4. Handout material was   Poor [ ]   Fair [ ]   Good [ ]
   Excellent [ ]
   Comment: _____

5. There was too much time spent on: _____
There was not enough time spent on: _____
There should have been coverage of: _____

6. I would/would not recommend this seminar to others because
_____

7. I would like to see a seminar on: _____
I think it ought to be _____ long.

8. My suggestions for improving this seminar are as follows: (Any general comments you would care to make are invited. Please use reverse side of this form if you need more space.)

_____

_____

_____

_____

_____

_____

Name (if you wish to supply it): _____

A PRE-PRESENTATION CHECKLIST

Many emergencies and other unexpected contingencies arise simply because we neglect to check everything prior to the time for delivering the presentation—the almost inevitable result of relying on memory to make all the last-minute checks. Even the most reliable memory has a way of deserting you when you are busy with all the last-minute duties. In any case, the following checklist is designed to help you to verify items prior to the actual presentation. Keep referring to this checklist (having adapted this to your own case and made copies to use) to see what items are not yet checked off. (Don't check them off until they are physical, accomplished reality).

Pre-Presentation Checklist

[ ]   Script/Cue Cards/Cheat Sheets: Ready (in my briefcase or on-site)

[ ]   Roster of Scheduled Attendees: Ready (in my briefcase or on-site)

Presentation Aids:

[ ]   Transparencies, Slides, etc: Ready (in briefcase)

[ ]   Posters, Other: Ready (shipped to site and verified as on-site)

Equipment:

[ ]   Projectors, Slide or Overhead: Ready on-site

[ ]   Blackboard Ready, with Chalk

[ ]   Flip Chart Board Ready, with Pens

[ ]   Models for Demonstration: Ready on-site

Handouts:

[ ]   Exercise Sheets: Ready, in briefcase or on-site

[ ]   Answer Sheets: Ready, in briefcase or on-site

[ ]   Manuals: Ready on-site

[ ]   Other Materials: Ready on-site

On-Site Logistics:

[ ]   Room Properly Prepared Classroom or Theater Style

[ ]   Coffee/Other Refreshments Ready

[ ]   Enough Chairs, Other Amenities

[ ]   Forms, Material for On-Site Registration in Place

[ ]   Administrator for On-Site Registration in Place

NOTE: This is a generalized checklist. Adapt it to your own situation and needs.

THE IN-HOUSE SPEAKER'S BUREAU

Many organizations operate an in-house speaker's bureau as an integral and important part of their public relations activity. In principle, it is a simple enough idea: It consists of establishing a capability and program for providing presenters for all occasions.

There are many uses to which a speaker's bureau can be put to support the PR efforts of the organization. Typically, organizations offering such services will supply speakers, without charge, for club and association meetings, conventions, trade shows, fairs, and sundry other events. For example, I was once a member of the in-house speaker's bureau of the Educational Science Division of U.S. Industries, and often addressed meetings of teachers and groups of industrial trainers to explain what we did as an organization and how we could help trainers and educators.

The function is usually established as part of the organization's marketing department, since PR is normally a marketing function. If a separate public relations office or function already exists, the speaker's bureau should be assigned there. However, many nonprofit organizations, such as government agencies and trade associations, also operate in-house speaker's bureaus and provide speakers for suitable occasions.

A first step in establishing such a capability is to create a roster of staff members who appear qualified as public speakers and capable of representing the organization well in that capacity. A policy must be written for the purpose, offering those listed on the roster a set of guidelines. Of course, the speakers' first obligation is to promote their organization and its purposes. Speakers must be indoctrinated suitably by the responsible manager, and lecture material supplied.

The lecture material may be a single script and administrative instructions or it may be a complete lecture guide containing various scripts written for predictable uses, as well as at least generalized script that can be readily adapted to each occasion. It depends on the nature of your organization and the specific purposes of the public relations office. But a lecture guide of some sort is definitely preferable as a means of maintaining a degree of consistency—remember that there will be various presenters used—and some sort of quality control.

In many cases, the speakers must be equipped with presentation aids—posters, slides, filmstrips, transparencies—

and portable projectors. Some organizations have public relations movies they have had made and show these to any group seeking relevant information.

To make the function successful in its purpose of providing suitable public relations for the organization, the availability of the speakers must be made known as widely as possible. Announcements should be sent out to all suitable organizations, for example, program chairpeople of associations—and releases prepared for newspapers, trade journals, and other periodicals.

A FEW REMINDERS

Until you have trained yourself to be ever conscious of a variety of important do's and don'ts of public speaking, it might be helpful for you to review the following list before each presentation you make.

Enunciation and Pronunciation

One of the most valuable bits of advice that the late popular singer Nat King Cole was given (from the late Cab Calloway) was to enunciate clearly. When next you hear a recording of one of Nat King Cole's renditions, note how clearly you can hear and understand each word. That is important in singing, but even more important in speaking publicly. When someone in an audience does not hear a speaker clearly, it is not always because that someone does not hear well or because the speaker does not speak loudly enough; often it is because the speaker does not enunciate words clearly.

Pronunciation is also important. Many of us know and use words that we learned in reading but never heard pronounced, and so we do not know how to pronounce them. Some words whose pronunciation I have found to confound even some well-educated individuals, for example, are *banal*, *ideology*, and *formidable*. In some cases, the "correct" pronunciation is debatable, with more than one pronunciation acceptable; in other cases, mispronouncing the word is damaging to your image and should be avoided. Hence, if you are not absolutely certain that you know the correct and accepted pronunciation, don't use the word at all, but find a suitable synonym.

Posture and Expression

Remember that you are on display when you are on the dais, and faults of posture are damaging to your image. Avoid the following, among many other characteristics that would stamp you as inexperienced and unprofessional on the platform:

- Slouching
- Leaning on the lectern or other support
- Bowing your head
- Standing with your hands in your pockets
- Toying with keys, your tie, or another object
- Putting your hand over your mouth when speaking
- Staring at your feet
- Standing rooted in one spot
- Being deadpan—totally inanimate in expression, as well as in motion
- Speaking in a monotone.

PICKING TOPICS AND TITLES

If you are to have broad appeal to an audience, you must give a good bit of thought to what interests most people. Many years ago the *Reader's Digest* reported that the most popular subjects were Abraham Lincoln, dogs, mothers, and medicine or health. From that they postulated that the ideal article would concern Lincoln's mother's doctor's dog. That is, of course, just a bit extreme, but the principle is sound enough.

It is not difficult to perceive what aspects of most subjects appeal to audiences generally. They are those that give us hope, touch us emotionally, have a great element of nostalgia, and evoke the pleasantly familiar. If you want to talk about careers, for example, focus on opportunity, not difficulties.

Unfortunately, too often those writing titles are more intent on being clever than on appealing to audiences. Forget about cleverness and forget about being cute. Concentrate on two objectives in writing a title for your presentation: Appeal and communication. (The appeal of the subject will be of no significance if the title does not explain the subject!) Writing a good title is an extreme case of writing a short advertisement: It is much more difficult than writing a long one; it is usually arrived at by starting with a long one. This is not to say, however, that the title must be only a few words. The effort to say it all in one or two words is one of the factors that often leads to poor titles that do not really communicate any useful information. Book titles illustrate this: The book *Five Acres* was converted from a mediocre success to a great success by changing its title to *Five Acres and Independence*. And in the case of other books, some with rather lengthy titles (*How to Prosper in the Coming Bad Years, How to Swim With the Sharks Without Being Eaten,* and *How to Succeed as an Independent Consultant*) have all been successful books.) "Short" is a relative term. This is the process:

1. Decide what the appeal and the message is to be.
2. Write it out completely, no matter how long.
3. Edit and rewrite it to size and final copy.

16

Anecdotes, Epigrams, and Humor

A mini-collection of condiments to add seasoning to your presentations. Season to taste.

A FEW SUGGESTIONS

There are many printed collections of humor and other items useful to spice up a presentation. They appear in large and small volumes, in paperback and cloth bound editions, many of them well known classics (e.g., Bartlett's *Familiar Quotations*, in print since 1882, with my own edition the 15th, published in 1980), others not at all known. One very useful book is *"A Funny Thing Happened on the Way to the Boardroom": Using Humor in Business Speaking*, by Michael Iapoce. Another rich source of jests, epigrams, wit, and famous quotations is the collected works of Shakespeare.

In this chapter, I offer a mini-collection of such items. It is neither a complete collection, nor organized in any special manner. It is intended only as a starter list—some of the materials I find humorous, insightful, and/or helpful in my own presentations. I hope you will find them equally helpful.

Those items which are represented to be direct quotations of others should be quoted precisely or, if paraphrasing, you should make that clear to your audience. You may find, however, that if you find a given epigram, witticism, or other item in more than one source, the wording may vary a bit, despite being attributed to an individual. Even Shakespeare's wording varies slightly in different editions of his work. You may also find that some items are attributed differently in one source than they are in another. In such cases, you will have to decide for yourself which is the most reliable or most accurate attribution and quotation.

On the other hand, you need feel no such restrictions in using unattributed anecdotes, jokes or other items. In fact, you should adapt the items to your own needs.

In general, it is best to draw on your own experience for anecdotes. (A few of those here are from my own experience, although modified slightly for literary purposes.) One reason for this chapter is to help you remember such incidents in your own history. Think back, as you study the items presented here (or elsewhere) and see if they do not provoke such memories.

There are three things you must remember about using humor in your presentation:

1. The humor must be woven into your material as part of it, and not dragged in by the ears just for the laugh. Use humor as part of your presentations, but don't tell jokes.

2. The item must be chosen for its appropriateness, that is, its adaptability to your presentation. Weave it in so that it *belongs* there and is a significant part of your presentation.

3. The humor comes about as a result of the punch line, which must come as something totally unexpected, a reversal of normal logic. In the days of the burlesque theater, for example, a common one-liner delivered as a put down by the comic to another performer was, "Did your mother have any children?" Another was, "You remind me of my brother—but he's alive."

Whether the item is a one-liner or a story, the humor usually depends on that snapper, the surprise twist that comes at the end of the line or the story. Many of the items you will read here are not intended to be humorous, and many that are intended as humor may strike you as not being especially funny. In fact, many *aren't* funny in their written form. But they can become humorous if you build them up in some way, as personal experiences of yours or of some friend or relative, and if you deliver the punch line properly.

Don't recite these items as they appear here, and most definitely do not simply read them to an audience. Rarely will one fit into your presentation properly without being tailored to your need. Find a way to adapt the item to help you make a point or to punctuate the point and make it more memorable.

Victor Borge, for example, although a most accomplished concert pianist, is even more noteworthy as a consummate wit, and his professional appearances are comedic. At the conclusion of one of his appearances on television, he stood before the large live audience and said, "I want to thank my sponsors for making this performance possible, and my family for making it necessary."

That snapper is easily adaptable to any presentation, although it is not proper to simply steal it without credit to its author, since you know who the author is. But it is easy to adapt it while still crediting the source of the witticism. In fact, it works much better when you mention the famous source:

> Ladies and gentlemen, I want to paraphrase the well known entertainer Victor Borge in thanking you for coming here tonight. But, like Mr. Borge, I also want to thank [the organization] for making this [presentation, seminar, other] possible, and my family for making it necessary.

That is appropriate if you are being paid a fee for speaking. But if you are speaking without fee, for example, as a duty that goes with your job, the snapper doesn't make a great deal of sense. However, you can still use the basic idea with a slightly different switch, such as ". . . and I want to thank my boss at [organization name] who asked me to volunteer to speak here tonight and who said that's how I could keep my job."

Another way to add meaning and appropriateness to your humor is to always attribute the action or the story, directly or indirectly, to someone you know or to your being there on the platform. (Have you noted how often a comedian sets up his or her first joke by saying, "A funny thing happened to me on my way to the theater tonight?") Use this idea as you build the story up. For example:

> There was a fellow named Joe Okie in my audience last week who came up to the dais to talk with me after my seminar. He was telling me about his early background, when he was a blue collar worker. He said he used to be a lumberjack, many years ago, when he was a young fellow, and he started to tell me how he was cutting lumber in the Sahara forest.
> "Wait a minute," I said. "The Sahara is a desert."
> He fixed me with a look of utter contempt. "Sure it's a desert," he said. *"Now."*
> Ladies and gentlemen, never mind how business was. Let's talk about *now*.

A single, key word may tie the anecdote to your point. Here is an example of that approach to working an anecdote into your material:

> I was walking down Connecticut Avenue in Washington, DC, one day last summer, when a man walking right in front of me suddenly keeled over. He had succumbed to the heat and humidity that is so typical of Washington summers. He just dropped. But before I could do anything, a woman who was a trained nurse, rushed over to see if she could help. She straightened his legs out, loosened his necktie, and took his jacket off.
> All the while she was talking soothingly to him. "There," she said, "it will be all right. Just relax."
> She rolled up his jacket and made a pillow of it, slipping it under his head. "That should help," she said. "Are your comfortable?"

The man looked at her and kind of shrugged. "Well," he answered, "I make a pretty good living."

The question is, are all of *you* "comfortable?" Do you all make a good living?

Note once again how the story is personalized, in this case as something you personally witnessed.

Of course, not everything has to be a lengthy anecdote. You can fit one-liners or brief quotations into your material in the same way. Suppose you are making the point that, instead of dissipating one's energy by trying to do too many things, one should focus one's effort on well-defined goals. You might say something such as the following:

If you strike out in all directions, you will find it difficult to get anywhere. You must pursue a more narrowly defined goal by uniting all these efforts. As Charles de Gaulle once said about the difficulty of uniting the French people, "Nobody can simply bring together a country that has 265 kinds of cheese."

With these admonitions in mind, use the following small potpourri of jokes, epigrams, quotations, and anecdotes by choosing the ones most readily adaptable to your needs, but do adapt them and do build them up in some manner so that the punch line has the right impact. As an introduction to this list, let me quote the late Gene Fowler:

- "If they haven't heard it before, it's original."
- Woodrow Wilson, twenty-eighth President of the United States, said he would require two weeks to prepare a 10-minute speech and one week for a one-hour speech, but could begin without notice to deliver a two-hour speech.
- "Do not tell me how hard you work. Tell me how much you get done." (James J. Ling)
- "Every great institution is the lengthened shadow of a single man." (Thomas Alva Edison)
- "When you paddle your own canoe, you can do the steering."

- "The doctor ordered him to eat more fruit, so he now has the bartender put a twist of lemon in his martinis."

- "Thank you, everyone, for that spontaneous apathy."

- I always keep a supply of stimulant handy, in case I see a snake, which I also keep handy.

- "The British have a remarkable talent for keeping calm, even when there is no crisis." (Franklin P. Adams)

- The late Dwight Morrow of Wall Street fame was told that a certain individual disliked him intensely. Morrow was puzzled. He could not account for the man's dislike. "I never did anything for him," he mused, in his efforts to understand the animosity.

- The strongman lifted weights, bent bars, and squeezed a lemon until it was an absolutely dry pulp. A natty little figure stepped forward, picked up the pulp, and squeezed an entire spoonful of additional juice out of it. He explained modestly that he was from the IRS.

- "A classic is something everybody wants to have read and no one wants to read." (Mark Twain)

- Genius does not wait on time and experience. Edgar Allen Poe had made his contributions to the world's literature before age 37. Napoleon had conquered Italy when he was 25 years old. Alfred Tennyson turned out his first volume at 18. Isaac Newton made some of his greatest discoveries before he was 25.

- Old age is no bar to accomplishment. Barbara McClintock won the Nobel Prize for medicine at age 81, and Subrahmanyan Chancrasekhar, 73, and William Fowler, 72, shared the prize for physics.

- A young student of music is supposed to have asked Mozart one day how to go about writing a concerto. Mozart responded by pointing out the youth of the inquirer, suggesting that he wait until he was a bit older. At that, the young man reminded Mozart that he had been composing since he was six years old.

"Yes," said Mozart, "but I didn't have to ask anyone how to do it."

- "A bore is a person who wants to talk when you want him to listen." (Ambrose Bierce)

- When someone told Dorothy Parker that Calvin Coolidge was dead, she asked, "How can they tell?"

- A wise judge, called upon to settle a dispute between two men over the division of a parcel of land they owned jointly, decreed that one man should divide the parcel into two, while the other should have first choice of the two portions.

- The late David Lloyd George was heckled during one of his campaign speeches by a man who made a sneering reference to Lloyd George's father as a peddler with a cart and donkey. Lloyd George paused and agreed that his father had been a poor man.

   "The cart has long disappeared," he noted, however, "but I see that the donkey is still with us."

- "If Lincoln were alive today, he'd be turning over in his grave." (Gerald R. Ford)

- I have a friend who has been stopped so often for speeding that the police sent him a season ticket.

- "Anyone who isn't thoroughly confused isn't thinking clearly." (Claire Booth Luce)

- "If I had known I was going to live this long, I would have taken better care of myself." (Wilson Warlick)

- "Now when I bore people at a cocktail party, they think it's their fault." (Henry Kissinger)

- If you are about to follow someone who had just made a brilliant presentation: "[X] and I agreed to swap speeches tonight, so here is his speech."

- Prizefighters don't do well at counting sheep when they have trouble falling asleep. They tend to jump up when the count reaches nine.

- He brightens up a room just by leaving it.

- Franklin D. Roosevelt's trusted aide and confidante, Harry Hopkins, was reportedly asked by Roosevelt where the population of the United States was most dense. "From the neck up," thought Hopkins.

- My brother broke his leg, but it could have been worse: It could have happened to me.

- What should a girl give a man who has everything? Encouragement.

- Adam was one man who knew that what he said was original.

- Kids certainly brighten up one's home; they never turn the lights off.

- I have my principles, but if you find them unacceptable I have some others.

- I didn't panic when one of the plane's engines caught fire because it wasn't on my side.

- The human brain is a marvel. It starts working the minute you open your eyes and doesn't stop until you get to your office.

- "I clean my diamonds with ammonia, my rubies with wine, and my sapphires with fresh milk," boasted Mrs. Newlyrich.
  "I don't bother," said her companion. "When mine get dirty I just throw them away."

- "Isn't it marvelous how those little chicks get out of their shells?" said he.
  "I think it is more marvelous how they get into them in the first place," said she.

- Pioneers get arrows in their backs, and missionaries wind up in the stew pot.

- The old man on his deathbed was asked by the clergyman if he would now renounce Satan.
  "No way," he said, "This is no time to make enemies."

- When Winston Churchill made his most famous speech, "We shall fight on the beaches, we shall fight on the landing grounds, we shall fight in the field and in the streets, we shall fight in the hills," Great Britain had just evacuated most of its army from France, leaving virtually all its equipment behind.

The Dean of Canterbury reported later that Churchill then murmured, with his hand held tightly over the microphone, "And we'll beat them over the head with beer bottles, for that's all we've got."

- His doctor pulled into Joe's service station with a flat tire, not long after he had hit Joe with a rather large bill for helping him through a simple case of indigestion. Joe diagnosed the doctor's automobile problem as "flatulence of the perimeter" and charged him accordingly.

- The lawyer was complaining bitterly about his latest case. "We got a pretty good settlement," he said, "but the client got almost as much out of the whole thing as I did."

- A cub reporter, sent to cover the great floods that had devastated Johnstown, Pennsylvania, sent back a portentous dispatch that began, "God sat on a hill overlooking Johnstown today."

  His editors wired back, "Forget the flood. Interview God."

- Critics are like eunuchs in a harem: They know how it is done; they have seen it done every day. But they can't do it themselves.

- That seaside town was so dull that one day the tide went out and never came back.

- Why does what Congress calls a slight tax increase cost you over $1,000, while what they call a significant tax reduction saves you $6.50?

- No one can make you feel inferior without your consent. (Eleanor Roosevelt)

- Success has ruined many a man. (Benjamin Franklin)

- Men occasionally stumble over the truth, but most of them pick themselves up and hurry off as if nothing had happened. (Winston Churchill)

- When George the waiter died, his widow went to a seance to summon his spirit. Soon there was a knocking on the table, and the widow said, "George? George? Speak to me."

    The voice replied, "Sorry, that's not my table."

- Three men ordered iced tea at a New York restaurant. As the waiter was departing, one man yelled after him, "Make sure it's a clean glass."

    When the waiter returned with the iced tea he asked, "Which one gets the clean glass?"

- He got quite a beating fighting for his girl's honor. She was determined to keep it.

- Anyone who goes to see a psychiatrist ought to have his head examined. (Samuel Goldwyn)

- That hotel is so exclusive that room service has an unlisted number.

- The best part about being a policeman is that the customer is always wrong.

- I know a guy who is so cautious he has roll bars on his speedboat.

- He doesn't drink very much; he spills most of it.

- The lawyer, seated behind his huge mahogany desk, listened carefully to the complaint of his new client, who was indignantly explaining his desire for justice.

    "Mr. Klien," he asked, "how much justice can you afford?"

- He got in to see the company president because he said it was a matter of life and death. It turned out he was an insurance salesman.

- Her husband decided to put some magic back into their marriage. He disappeared.

- Joe College borrowed his roommate's raincoat so he wouldn't get his roommate's new suit wet.

- The food there is so bad that pygmies stop by to dip their darts in the soup.

- Why is it that when you retire and time doesn't matter a great deal to you any more they give you a watch?

- The waiter came over and got his order promptly, but when he finally got back with the order, the patron looked puzzled. "Are you sure you're my waiter?" he asked. "I expected a much older man."

- Can you believe that someone, someday will call these "the good, old days?"

- If you really want to hear promptly from your son at college write and tell him you're enclosing $50 but don't enclose the money.

- The bride looked stunning and the groom looked stunned.

- A government official, reviewing the stacks of brochures from a multitude of companies competing for lucrative government contracts, was heard to comment, "The bigger the name, the smaller the company."

- The patron ordered a Maine lobster. When the waiter brought the lobster, the patron grabbed him by the arm.

  "Wait a minute. This lobster has only one claw. What kind of lobster is this?"

  The waiter shrugged. "Lobsters get in fights with each other and they lose claws sometimes."

  The diner nodded. "I understand. So why did you bring me the loser? Bring me the winner!"

- John D. Rockefeller was reported to have advised others, as a road to success, to observe some successful entrepreneur and do likewise. But many successes were based on the courage to be original and different. Woolworth's idea was the five and ten cent store. Henry Ford decided on a light, cheap car and only one model. Montgomery Ward .was the pioneer in the unconditional, money-back guarantee.

- Success does not come easily, especially to original thinkers. George Westinghouse had great difficulty getting his air brakes taken seriously, much less accepted. The experts of his day sneered at Charles Kettering's effort to invent the automobile self-starter, as other experts had sneered at Thomas Alva Edison for his foolish idea of incandescent lighting.
- Wagner's music is better than it sounds. (Mark Twain)
- Don't ever steal from another author. That's plagiarism. Steal from 50 or 60 other authors. That's research.
- I got a postcard from a friend of mine while he was on vacation. It said, "Having a wonderful time. Wish I could afford it."
- Winston Churchill was not very fond of Clement Atlee, and when someone commented on Atlee's alleged modesty, Churchill responded that Atlee had a great deal to be modest about.
- "The winds and waves are always on the side of the ablest navigators." (Edward Gibbon)
- It was reported that George Bernard Shaw sent Winston Churchill two passes to the opening of a new play he had written. An accompanying note invited Churchill to bring a friend ". . . if you have one."

  Churchill responded that he could not make it opening night, but he would be pleased to attend the second showing ". . . if there is one."
- The harder you work, the luckier you get. (Gary Player)
- Herbert Hoover, thirty-first President of the United States, donated to charitable causes every cent of federal salary paid him during many periods of federal service, ranging over 47 of his 90 years. He had made his fortune early as a mining engineer, and thus acknowledged what he termed "a great debt" to his country.

- It was George Bernard Shaw who pointed out how unfortunate it was that the blessing of youth was wasted on the young.
- When someone gets something for nothing, someone else gets nothing for something.
- "Few people think more than two or three times a year. I have made an international reputation for myself by thinking once or twice a week." (George Bernard Shaw)
- "A sign of celebrity is often that his name is worth more than his services." (Daniel J. Boorstin)
- "The only time you realize you have a reputation is when you're not living up to it." (José Iturbi)
- "Business has only two basic functions—marketing and innovation." (Peter F. Drucker)
- George McGovern, long-time veteran of official life in Washington, DC, observed that the longer the title, the less important the job.
- "One man with courage makes a majority." (Andrew Jackson)
- Senator Theodore Green, a Rhode Island Democrat, found a way to save money while winning votes for his party: When campaigning, he did not tip waiters, taxi drivers, and others, but cautioned them instead, "Be sure to vote Republican."
- "No one ever went broke underestimating the intelligence of the American People." (H. L. Mencken)
- H. L. Mencken often referred to the American people as the "booboisie."
- "The "C" students run the world." (Harry S Truman)
- About a hot political campaign Clare Booth Luce said, "The politicians were talking themselves red, white, and blue in the face."
- Everett M. Dirksen, Republican Senator from Illinois, mused one day, "A billion here and a billion there, and pretty soon we're talking about real money."

- Everett Dirksen told the story of a man whose father had been hanged, and who was understandably reluctant to confess the fact when filling out an application for insurance. He reported that his father had died as a result of "participating in a public function when the platform gave way."

- "An army of stags led by a lion is more formidable than an army of lions led by a stag." (Plutarch)

- About his role as the leader who inspired his people so much during the darkest days of the Second World War, Winston Churchill said, "it was the nation that had the lion's heart. I had the luck to be called upon to give the roar."

- "This job has done wonders for my paranoia. Now I *really* have enemies." (Henry Kissinger)

- "Difficulty is the one excuse that history never accepts." (Edward R. Murrow)

- A bystander heckled Al Smith, during one of Smith's speeches, with, "Tell them all you know. It won't take long."

  Smith retorted, "I'll tell them all we both know; it won't take any longer."

- At a well-attended cocktail party, a thorough bore, Bill Jones, observed to a pretty young thing, "I am my own worst enemy."

  Someone who knew Jones well happened to overhear the remark and murmured, "Not while I am alive you are not."

- In Israel, in order to be a realist you must believe in miracles. (David Ben-Gurion)

- John F. Kennedy was considered by many to be quite young to be President, and he was well aware of that sentiment. He remarked that even if he served two terms in office he might still be at an "awkward age": ". . . too old to begin a new career and too young to write my memoirs."

- Werner von Braun, the German rocket expert who headed up the rocket program at the NASA Flight Center at Huntsville, Alabama, stirred up something of a hornet's nest with a thoughtless answer. He had been asked by a reporter if he thought humans could live on the moon.

  "Why not?" he responded. "If you can live in Huntsville, you can live on the moon."

- It was also Werner von Braun who greeted a bunch of newcomer scientists of NASA by welcoming them to the "mushroom club," to great laughter by most of those listening. Asked by several of the newcomers to explain what the "mushroom club" was, von Braun explained that they all belonged to that "club" because NASA kept them in the dark most of the time, except when they opened the door briefly to shovel in some manure on them.

- The advertisement said "Popular Prices." The customer looked at the goods displayed and thought all the prices far too high. "You call these popular prices," she demanded of the proprietor.

  He shrugged. "We like them," he said.

- As the train went roaring past a huge pasture in the heart of Texas, a traveler sitting by the window whistled. "Wow! Look at all those steers out there," he said.

  A man sitting beside him said, "Yes, that is large herd. There are seventy-two hundred and seventeen animals out there."

  The first man's mouth dropped wide open. "How did you know that?" he asked. "How could you know that?"

  "Easy," said the second man. "Just count the legs and divide by four."

- The captain of a freighter was taken ill one day, and the first mate had to take over command for the day. He got out the ship's log to note the fact, and he noticed that every day for the previous two weeks the captain had made an entry: "First mate drunk today."

The first mate was incensed. He stewed about it for a long time. Then he was inspired. He seized a pen and wrote in the day's log, "Captain sober today."

- A newly graduated and licensed young lawyer joined a prestigious, well-established law firm. An older, thoroughly experienced member of the firm was assigned to indoctrinate the firm's newest lawyer.

  "As a practical matter," said the old timer, "when you have the facts on your side, you pound the jury, but when you have the law on your side, you pound the judge."

  "I understand," said the fledgling. "But what if I don't have either the facts or the law on my side?"

  "That's easy," smiled his mentor. "When you don't have either the facts or the law on your side, you pound the table."

- No experienced holdup man in Washington, DC, ever says to a victim there, "Give me your money or I will blow your brains out." That is the wrong choice to offer anyone in Washington because it is well known that you need money to get along there, but you don't need brains.

- Old timers in Washington, DC, often point out to newcomers that if you want a friend in Washington, buy a dog.

- The late Bertrand Russell recalled that he had been confined in Great Britain as a conscientious objector during the first World War. He stood before a clerk answering questions asked by the clerk, who was reading the questions from and recording the answers on a printed form.

  He answered each question solemnly and routinely enough, without incident, until the clerk asked his religion.

  To that question he responded, "Agnostic."

  The clerk paused, looking puzzled and studying Russell quizzically. Then: "Hmmm, never heard of that one." Then, returning to the form on the desk before him, the clerk shrugged and murmured, "Well, I guess we all believe in the same God."

- Bertrand Russell also related a conversation with a French nun, who mentioned that she always wore a covering, even when taking a bath. That puzzled Russell a bit.

  "Surely," he said, "you bathe in private in a closed room?"

  "Ah," said the nun, "but one is never alone. You forget *le bon dieu*."

  Russell recalls that he said no more, refraining from asking the nun why she thought God could see through her bathroom walls but not through her bathing gown.

Appendix

Publications and Associations of Interest

There are many publications of interest—books, magazines, and newsletters. The following is by no means a complete list, but should be helpful in expanding your resources generally and your awareness of what is happening in the world of public speaking.

Books

Berg, Karen, and Andrew Gilman, with Edward P. Stevenson, *Get to the Point*, Bantam Books, New York, 1990.

Bartlett, John, *Familiar Quotations*, 15th Ed., Little, Brown and Company, Boston, 1980.

Boyland, Bob, *What's Your Point?* Warner Books, New York, 1988.

Burgett, Gordon, and Mike Frank, *Speaking for Money*, Communication Unlimited, Carpinteria, 1985.

Christopher & Victor Navasky, *The Experts Speak*, Pantheon Books, New York, 1984.

Delton, Judy, *The 29 Most Common Writing Mistakes and How to Avoid Them*, Writer's Digest Books, Cincinnati, 1985.

Detz, Joan, *How to Write & Give a Speech*, St. Martin's Press, New York, 1984.

Hoff, Ron, *"I Can See You Naked,"* Andrews and McNeel, Kansas City, 1988.

Holtz, Herman, *Speaking for Profit,* John Wiley, New York, 1985.

Humes, James C., *Podium Humor,* Harper & Row, Perennial Library edition, New York, 1985.

Iapoce, Michael, *A Funny Thing Happened on the Way to the Boardroom: Using Humor in Business Speaking,* John Wiley, New York, 1988.

Kirkpatrick, A.L., *Complete Speaker's and Toastmaster's Desk Book,* Parker Publishing Co., West Nyack, 1981.

Martel, Myles, Ph.D., *The Persuasive Edge,* Ballantine Books, New York, 1984, 1989.

McMahon, Ed, with Warren Jamieson, *Superselling,* Prentice Hall, New York, 1989.

Nelson, Robert B., and Jennifer Wallick, *Making Effective Presentations,* Scott Foresman and Comany, Glenview, 1990.

Peoples, David A., *Presentations Plus,* John Wiley, New York, 1988.

Prochnow, Herbert V. and Herbert V. Prochnow, Jr., *The Public Speaker's Treasure Chest,* Fourth Ed., Harper & Row, New York, 1986.

Qubein, Nido R., *Communicate Like a Pro,* Prentice Hall, Englewood Cliffs, 1983.

Shook, Robert L., *The Perfect Sales Presentation,* Bantam Books, New York, 1990.

Smith, Terry C., *Making Successful Presentations: A Self-Teaching Guide,* 2nd Edition, John Wiley, New York, 1990.

Tomlinson, Gerald, *Speaker's Treasury of Political Stories, Anecdotes & Humor,* Prentice Hall, Englewood Cliffs, 1990.

Turner, Stuart, *The Public Speaker's Bible,* Thorson's Publishing Group, Wellingsborough, Northamptonshire, England, 1988.

Walters, Dottie and Lillet, *Speak and Grow Rich*, Prentice Hall, Englewood Cliffs, 1989.

Wheeler, Elmer, *How To Sell Yourself to Others*, Cornerstone Library, New York, 1974.

White, Rolf B., *The Great Business Quotations*, Dell Publishing Co., New York, 1986.

Wilder, Claudyne, *The Presentations Kit*, John Wiley, New York, 1990.

Wohlmuth, Ed, *The Overnight Guide to Public Speaking*, Running Press, Philadelphia, 1983, 1990.

Newsletters

Sharing Ideas, P.O. Box 1120, Glendora, CA 91740.

Speechwriter's Newsletter, Lawrence Ragan Communications, Inc., 407 S. Dearborn Street, Chicago, IL 60605.

Associations

American Society for Training and Development (ASTD), P.O. Box 5307, Madison, WI 53705.

International Platform Association, 2564 Berkshire Road, Cleveland Heights, OH 44106.

National Speakers Association (NSA), 4747 N. 7th Street, Suite 310, Phoenix, AZ 85014.

Professional Speakers Association, 3540 Wilshire Blvd, Suite 310, Los Angeles, CA 90010.

Toastmaster's International, 220 N. Grand Avenue, Santa Ana, CA 92711.

Index